Helen Corey's
Food from Biblical Lands

A Culinary Trip to the Land of Bible History

Feast of the Transfiguration, August 6, is celebrated by Reverend Father George Rados, Potomac, Maryland, as he blesses a grape arbor at the home of Helen Corey. St. George Orthodox parishioners witnessed the blessing as they attended a garden party in his honor.

The Very Reverend Father Rados and Helen Corey

Father Rados Enjoying the Cookout

Father Rados with Parishoners Looking On

Father Rados blesses the grape arbor, assisted by Reverend Deacon Elias Corey

Published by Echo Point Books & Media
Brattleboro, Vermont
www.EchoPointBooks.com

All rights reserved.
Neither this work nor any portions thereof may be reproduced, stored in a retrieval system, or transmitted in any capacity without written permission from the publisher.

Copyright © 1989, 2016 by Helen Corey

Helen Corey's Food from Biblical Lands
ISBN: 978-1-62654-389-8 (casebound)

Photographs: pages VI, 28, 100, 133 by Cassell Productions; kibby and bread by Bob Kadel

Arabic script by Anise Kassis

Iterior design by Jane Ford

Cover design by Adrienne Núñez
Editorial and proofreading assistance by Ian Straus, Echo Point Books & Media

MOST REVEREND
METROPOLITAN PHILIP
PRIMATE

RT. REV. BISHOP ANTOUN
AUXILIARY

MOST REVEREND
ARCHBISHOP MICHAEL, AUXILIARY
2656 PEMBERTON DRIVE
TOLEDO, OHIO 43606
(419) 535-1390

Antiochian Orthodox Christian Archdiocese
OF NORTH AMERICA
358 MOUNTAIN ROAD
ENGLEWOOD, NEW JERSEY 07631
201 871-1355

1996

Miss Helen Corey
146 S.E. 23rd
Terre Haute, Indiana 47803

Dear Helen,

Grace and peace in the Name of our Lord.

It gives us much pleasure to endorse your new cookbook. This volume contains such a wealth of information for those who wish to properly prepare Middle Eastern cuisine. It is also the only book of its kind which faithfully portrays the religious and cultural significance of the various foods which our people have eaten since the dawn of time.

We highly recommend that your book be used in all of our Antiochian Orthodox parishes.

With our sincere blessings and best wishes,

Metropolitan PHILIP
Primate
Antiochian Orthodox Christian Archdiocese
of North America

MP:km

The late Metropolitan Philip always enthusiastically endorsed Helen Corey's cookbooks, as evidenced by this letter.

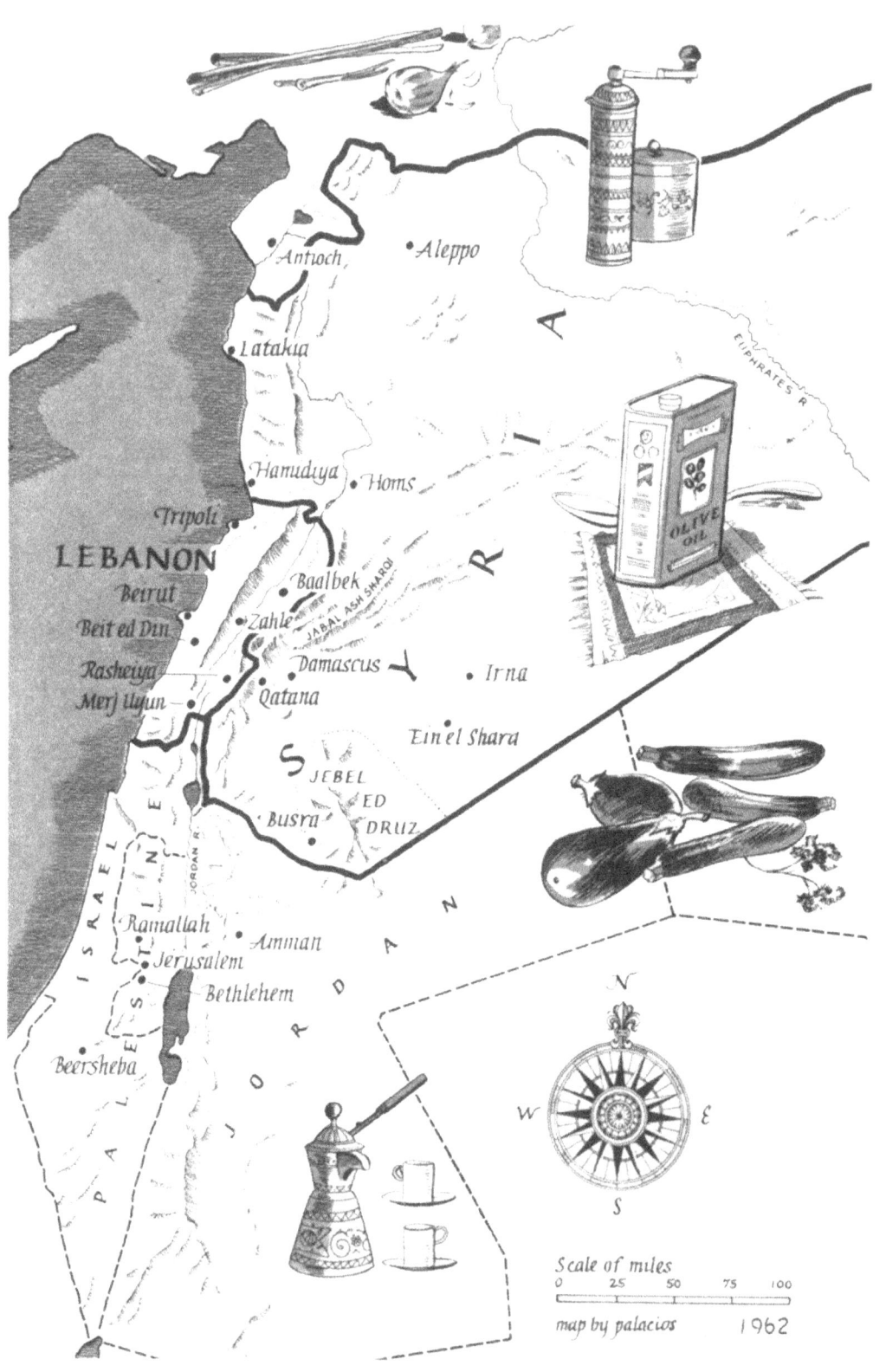

DEDICATION

With love and admiration, I dedicate this book to my late mother *Maheeba* (Mabel). It was always a learning experience watching her artistry of preparing foods fit for the Kings. Constant dinner parties at our home and entertaining the Hierarchy of the Antiochian Orthodox Church down through the years has added to the excitement of presenting this text and recipes for your reading and cooking pleasure.

100 years young on August 15, 1995, *a blessed day,* she continued to amaze everyone with her keen mind and knowledge of current and historical events. She was often asked what she did to keep herself healthy and beautiful (not a wrinkle on her skin). She was a blessing to us and taught us a valuable lesson with her biblical stories and health-style, and the open-door policy where we break bread with everyone as we practice the Arabic proverb **"God Fed You—Eat and Feed."**

Always the first in the city to plant a favorite of all Middle Eastern people, fava beans *ful,* here she is with freshly harvested fava beans.

ACKNOWLEDGMENTS

To my late sister Kate, a superb cook, for helping me to review many of these recipes for accuracy. A grandmother of 10 and loved by all, she was known for her mouth-watering meat pies *sfeeha* and her Syrian fried doughnuts *zalabee*. Always at the helm of church festivals kneading the dough for these delicacies, children and adults devoured them as fast as they were made.

A special thanks to the Embassy of Syria for providing me with data for the historical "Journey to Syria" and to the Minister of Tourism in Syria for his gracious praises on my books. And to Massoud Malouf, Attache' to the Lebanese Embassy and his wife Janet who hosted an elegant party in my honor with Mr. Malouf's sister Sonia from Lebanon preparing a sumptuous unforgettable Lebanese meal topped off with *Samke Harra*, recipe included in this updated edition.

To my brother Bob who handles calls and mail for my cookbooks, (known to everyone as "cuz" on the golf course) I couldn't handle it without him. A generous person with everyone he knows, he is always there taking care of Mom's needs. He threw a fabulous 100th birthday party for her where he prepared bar-b-q and all the trimmings for 400 guests at our home in Terre Haute.

A special thank you to dearest friend Laurice Neam, a great cook of Arlington, Virginia, always on hand to see that I get to embassy parties, for hosting many parties in my behalf and for opening her home to me. I could never make a trip to Washington, D.C. without Laurice being on hand taking me to my various book signing and lectures.

My thanks to Al Joseph, a St. Jude Hospital Board member, who has enriched the lives of so many, including mine, in a special way. My gratitude goes to him for his constant support.

And to the Federation of Syrian-Lebanese American Clubs throughout the country for their warm hospitality including me in their cultural activities for cooking classes I conducted at their conventions. And especially to Ruth Ann Skaff of St. Jude Children's Hospital whose enthusiasm for our heritage spearheaded the classes along with other cultural activities.

My gratitude to many friends from Palestine, Jordan, Egypt, and Morocco and those around the country that have opened their homes to me giving me an insight to their cuisine. My thanks to my traveling companions Ginny and Nellie Maloley for their constant help and Nellie's photo shoots at my cooking classes. They make it easier for me to handle my many assignments.

To dear friends Zeldia Hanna, Marie and Ann Ajamie for their devotion, loyalty and assistance always at various functions taking care of serving lines, replenishing foods, and keeping the kitchen organized, and to Lorraine Ajamie, my thanks for making herself available at a moment's notice to take photos when I'm cooking up some new dishes.

To Meena Khoury from Beit Zahur, Palestine for providing me with many items from the Middle East to use at my parties and in this book. And to Alice and Edith Mesalam for allowing me to use their exquisite mother of pearl tables and other artifacts for photos I used at my workshop for the Smithsonian Institute.

A warm and heart-felt thank you to Anita and Sam Cracchiolo of Boca Raton for the lavish and magnificent dinners in my honor. And to the many friends throughout the country who have hosted parties in my honor, I'm deeply grateful and blessed having you in my life.

To Father Antony Gabriel, astute in world and religious history, goes my thanks for providing me with religious material for television shows. To Bishop John Abdalah, editor of *The Word,* articles that are truly my "Bible."

As one of his flock among the multitude, I am grateful to Metropolitan Archbishop Philip whose message serves as my constant reminder that ours is a world of love, mercy and compassion for mankind everywhere. I've been truly blessed by having the opportunity to "break bread" with His Eminence and all of these priests; I am grateful to them for "feeding" me with their endless knowledge of the history of Christianity and Orthodoxy.

I'm deeply grateful for your many letters and phone calls. You've made my mother *Maheeba* a very happy lady with your letters and phone calls, telling her that she reminds you of your mother or grandmother. And especially to all of you for your bountiful words of praise on the recipes and photos in the 24 editions and current updated edition of The Art of Syrian Cookery, and your insurmountable letters of wanting more books to share with your children and friends, you've been my inspiration and to you I'm deeply grateful.

PREFACE

Arabic cooking is like Arabic dancing - vivid, exotic, enchanting. Moistened with olive oil and butter, flavorsome meat and rice rolled in cabbage and grape leaves, salads glistening with lemon juice and olive oil, succulent poultry smothered with a zesty sumac, rice and orzo uniquely standing on end in a clarified butter, stuffed summer squash in a tantalizing mint-yogurt sauce, and many irresistible desserts are just an inkling of some of the most nutritious and versatile foods that take you on an adventure of eating habits of Middle Eastern people since Biblical times.

And herewith is a description of some of these foods shown on the opposite page:

Top row:	Fatayer laban, Fatayer Za'tar or Mana'eesh, Fatayer spinach, Baklawa tray, Ricotta pastries
2nd row:	Arabic breads, Candied figs, Lahum nee, Turkish coffee
3rd row:	Olives, Pickled turnips, Kibby qras, Homos bi tahini, Joban cheese
4th row:	Sfeeha, Kibby nee, Pickled garlic eggplant
5th row:	Miqtha, (syrian cucumber) Broiled lemony chicken on a bed of Rice-orzo, Tabooley health salad
6th row:	Grape leaves stuffed with lamb and rice
7th row:	Stuffed squash cooked in Yogurt sauce, Mowaseer and Shish kebab on bed of Cracked wheat and Chick peas, Cheese with Olives.

This book includes foods from many regions in the Middle East. There is a great similarity in many of the foods, but some of the preparation and seasonings differ from city to city just as dialects differ.

A part of my heritage, these recipes have been handed down from mother to daughter for generations and followed by instinct . . . a little of this, a pinch of that . . . and flavored to please the palate, though the ingredients were never accurately measured.

In gathering these recipes from my mother *Maheeba*, she recalled many scenes of her native land, of certain *haflis*, (parties)...of the rich aroma of Arabic coffee poured into a demitasse, of the historical background of Arabic script and the makings of exquisite damask cloth.

With an influx of people from many lands that have come to America, there is a new surge of those who have changed their eating habits, learning that these Middle Eastern foods are filled with the healthiest of all ingredients since time-immemorial. Topping many foods in the world for low-calorie, protein-filled delicacies is the health salad of the entire Middle East *Tabooley* and *Laban* (yogurt) in salads and in sauces; *Falafel*, a blend of chick peas, spices, and cumin powder, and a favorite appetizer *tahini* a sesame paste that is also smothered on baked fish sprinkled with pine nuts... and so much more with the scent of spices enticing you into a world of foods you will long remember.

A loaf of *khobaz* (bread) with some olives, *joban,* and *labanee* nurtures the soul...and as you enter our kitchen, you'll whet your appetites to fried *kibby* sizzling in a skillet, the aroma of onions and garlic sauteing in pure olive oil, *baba ghanouj* (eggplant with tahini) *fatayer sabanigh and za'tar* and a tempting array of *maza*.

In addition, I wanted to share with you many of the symbolic and religious significance of foods served on feast days of the Orthodox church; Easter, Epiphany, the preparation of bread for the Holy Communion. **In keeping with today's health guidelines included in this book is a complete section providing you with a healthy variety of meatless dishes.**

Interspersed throughout this book are chapter and verse references from the Old and New Testament of foods eaten since the dawn of time. May you find nourishment of soul and body as you read this text and prepare these foods that are being acclaimed as today's healthiest foods by leading nutritionists throughout the world.

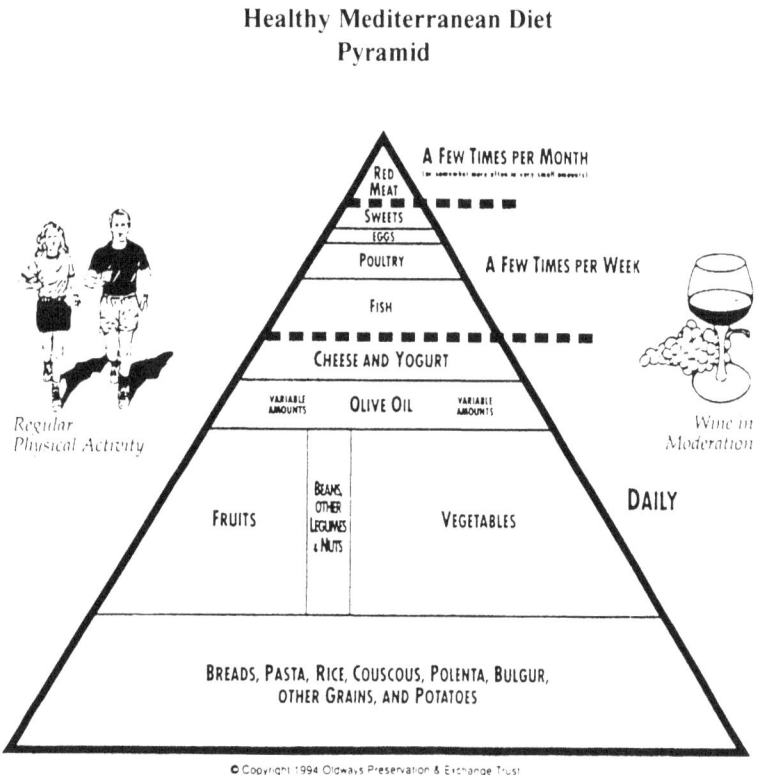

The Middle Eastern way of eating closely resembles that of the Mediterranean region. People from these countries eat a healthful diet rich in grain foods - breads, pasta, rice, bulgur, couscous, lentils, legumes, fruits and vegetables. These are complex carbohydrate rich foods needed for energy. These foods are also rich in valuable vitamins, minerals and fiber. Most of the fat in this diet comes from olive oil, which is monounsaturated and better for your heart.

And like every diet based on balance, variety and moderation, the Middle Eastern diet leaves room for occasional sweets and dessert.

Kim Galeaz, registered dietitian and nutrition consultant

CONTENTS

Recommendation of Metropolitan Philip Saliba I
Dedication III
Acknowledgments IV
Introduction - From the Land of My Ancestors XI
Spices and Herbs XV
Arabic Menus XVIII
Appetizers and Cheeses 1
The Making of Laban (Yogurt) 7
Kishik 9
Soups 11
Salads 17
Olive Oil and Olives 25
Mansef parties 29
Meats of the Middle East - *Mahrajan* 31
Game, Poultry and Dressings 41
Couscous 49
Wheat and Kibby 51
Omelets 57
Vegetables 59
Pickles 72
Breads and Pies 77
Beverages 87
Candied Fruits and Preserves 91
Pastries and Desserts 97
Fish 110

Lenten Foods 115
    Fasts Prescribed by the Eastern Orthodox Church 115
    Lenten Pies 117
    Lenten Kibby and Falafel 119
    Lentil dishes 121
    Wheat and Vegetable Dishes 123
    Lenten Desserts 129

Meatless Menus 131

Traditions and Foods of the Orthodox Catholic Church 133
    Holy Altar Bread and Holy Communion 133
    Easter Eggs 134
    Boiled Wheat for Requiem Liturgy 136
    Feast Days and Menus 136
    The Feast of Epiphany 139

Passover..14 109,135

Glossary...141
Recipe index, English...145
Arabic recipe index..149
Relating to Religion...143

Author's late brother Bob Corey was always on hand offering a maza platter to guests, along with a quaff of coffee, in his generous open door policy.

INTRODUCTION

From The Land of my Ancestors

From the shores of the Mediterranean - land of the Son of God, land of Prophets, Patriarchs, and Apostles - throughout Syria and Lebanon, the same generous hospitality and an open door await the guest. And whether they be Syrians, Lebanese, Palestinians, Jordanians, Egyptians, Saudi Arabians and all parts of the Middle East, Arab hospitality is obviously inborn. On meeting them, their generosity is evident. From the moment you enter a home, you are greeted with *marhaba or ahlan wa sahlan*, a welcome that embraces you as a friend making you feel most comfortable and relaxed.

The familiar phrase *"Nishkor Allah wa-silt bil salami"* (Praise the Lord you arrived safely) is repeated by host and relatives as they receive visitors from abroad.

As introductions are made, one becomes aware that many proper names are derived from names of the Deity. For instance, my brother's name is *Abdullah* (Albert) which means servant of God. My father *Mkhyal* (Michael) is addressed *"Boo Abdullah"* (father of Albert) and my mother is addressed *"Im Abdullah"* (mother of Albert). Arabic-speaking people are taught from early childhood to show respect for their parents and their elders. A young person never addresses an elder by his proper name, but rather as *"Umtee"* (Auntie) or *"Umee"* (Uncle).

Early morning visiting is usual as everyone gets up before dawn while the air is fresh and cool. A brisk walk to a friend's home gives one a chance to view a paradise of fruit trees. As the guest arrives, coffee and sun-ripened apricots, grapes, and honey-filled figs **(Deut. 8:7,8)** are placed on tables inlaid with mother-of-pearl. A few hours later at home, regular breakfast consists of coffee, olives, *za-tar with sumac*, scrambled eggs covered with *kamoun* (cumin powder), *joban and qareeshee* (cheeses) and freshly baked hot loaves of *talamee and marquq* breads that nurture the soul.

In the entire Arab world this bread is considered the staff of life; *eish* is always round, depicting the eternal circle, the *talamee* is thick; the *mraqud* is hollow and used for all kinds of fillings; and the *marquq* is paper-thin, but all of them are round. Appetizing morsels of *lahum mishwee* (lamb on skewers) are placed in the bread and served with a side dish of *laban* which is scooped up into the bread. What is known popularly in America today as Pita Bread, has been made for centuries by Arabic people, known as *kmaj* or *mra-qud*. Sealing friendships with the "breaking of bread" has been a tradition since ancient times and practiced today in homes of Middle Eastern people. The religious significance of bread can be found in the chapter on Holy Oblation. Taking the place of water on some occasions is *shraab* (a mixture of fruit juices) or *nbeeth* (wine served in silver cups inscribed with Arabic mottoes). Many other earthen vessels serve as household containers for oil, honey, wine, rice, wheat, pickles, flour and olives. **(Num. 18:12)**

In Damascus, many bazaars fill the streets and alleys of a whole section of the city. Vendors, yelling *"halee dirsak ya walad"* (food for sweet tooth, young one), sell *halawa* (a delicious paste made with sesame seeds and *qathamee* (roasted chick peas). A visitor can walk down *Souqel (street of) Bezourieh* in Damascus and see many vendors. Nearby on the *Souq Arsouniyah and Mahidien* are shops jammed with *nargilehs*, hardware and Arabic instruments.

Scribes sit on oriental rugs in front of buildings in Damascus mastering the difficult art of gracefully written Arabic script. Writing from the right side to the left, little marks placed above and below a word indicate vowels. Once one learns expressions that only come from a language as rich as that in Arabic, they fall under the spell of the most powerful method of expression in Arabic songs and poetry.

The wisdom in this expressive language constantly fascinates me. Making notes and studying proverbs I had started my own collection from my Uncle, the late Right Reverend George Ghannam. With pen in hand at our church conventions, I manage to gain more knowledge from those articulate in the field of proverbs. So I penned a few more that I gleaned from Father Joseph Rahal of Toronto and Father Ted Ziton of Canton, Ohio. What a meaningful proverb that every Arabic family practices daily:

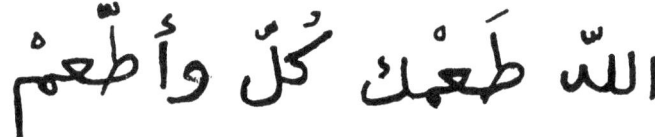

ALLAH TA' MAK; KOL WIT 'UM;   GOD FED YOU; EAT AND FEED

Without any hesitation in putting food on the table instantly for any amount of guests and for those in need, we believe strongly in this proverb:

AKEL WAHID BE QUDI THNINE :   A MEAL FOR ONE IS ENOUGH FOR TWO.

An exotic type of entertainment has been brought to America from the Middle East. At *sahras* (parties) guests are treated to Arabic rhythms poured forth by *derbukkis* (drums), reed, and lute. Dancers whirl and sway to the music, and the guests join the dance of the *dubkee*. Troubadours of the twelfth and thirteenth centuries accompanied their ballads with the lute, an original Arabic instrument called *il oud*. Al Ghazali, a philosopher wrote: "He whom the spring with its blossoms does not move, nor the lute with its strings, is corrupt of nature."

Prior to a wedding, festivity lasts for a week at the home of a bride. Women take turns singing *zalagheet* (wedding songs) with verses such as *"Ah wee, ahla sahla bil thyoof, ah wee, nisqee il ahal wal thyoof"* (welcome to the guests, a toast to the parents of the bride and groom). Guests are served mounds of pastries, pistachios, almonds, sunflower and pumpkin seeds. The candy-coated almond signifies a sweet and prosperous life.

The tradition lives on in my city of Terre Haute, Indiana where everyone joins in the response of *"lulla, lulla leish"* as Kate Malooley and Mary Ann Tanoos sing *zalagheet*.. Guests are eager to find a spot in the *dubkee* line as Terre Haute native Joe Sabb, Jr. brings out the *oud* while Ferris Shahadey, Jr. and caterer George Azar beat the *derbukkis*. And the dancing goes on with fervor throughout the night just as it does when renouned *oudist* Emil Kassis of Washington, D.C. plays at Danny Thomas's St. Jude conventions and throughout the country at many *haflis*, with Al Mansour and George Sabbag leading the dubkee lines. And Queen of the *dubkee* Alice Mesalem in Indianapolis and King of the *dubkee* Michele Shahin of Windsor, Ontario have the crowd joining in this lively dance.

In the Middle East, one day prior to the wedding, gifts of goats and lamb are sent to the bridegroom's home to be made ready for feasting hundreds of guests. Meats are cooked all night long in a huge *khal-qeenee* (kettle). *Kibby* heads the tempting array of foods. Platters filled with *Roz* (rice dotted with browned orzo), *Sheikh il mihshee* (eggplant stuffed with lamb and pine nuts) and *Waraq' inib mihshee* (diced lamb and rice in grape leaves). If the wedding takes place in the summer, foods are placed in trays and laid out on sheets on the roof. Guests take turns climbing the stone steps to partake of the feast. A familiar saying to the couple at the end of the wedding is *"Niq-sha' lak Arees"* (May you be blessed with a boy).

The home's flat rooftop serves many purposes. When wheat is washed, it is spread on the roof to dry under the sun, placed in an earthen barrel, and stored for winter provisions. In the same storeroom are bunches of garlic and onions, dates, figs and apricots strung together, all suspended from the ceiling.

These dried fruits are sold at colorful market places of Syria and Lebanon. Especially tempting are the varieties of apricots grown around Damascus. The apricot is pressed, dried and sold in thin sheets called *Qamardeen*. An extensive variety of nuts is available, along with cheeses and breads covered with sesame seeds or topped with golden-brown chick-peas. Used in many foods is the *snoober* (pine nut) which comes from the umbrella pine cones. The cones are placed on the rooftop and then the nuts fall out and are ready to be eaten or stored with the other provisions.

The Syrian's daily habits and conversation center around the church. It is unheard of to leave on a journey without making the sign of the Cross and saying *"Be ism Il Ab, Wal Ibin, Wal Rooh Il Qodos,* (In the name of the Father, the Son, and the Holy Spirit)."

The greeting *"Ahlan wa sahlan"* awaits you in the homes of second and third generation families of Syrian-Lebanese descent in America and whatever country they live in - and on your departure you will be given an often-heard blessing from parent to child, and from friend to friend *"Allah koon ma'eck"* (God be with you.)

We are indeed a happy, warm, loving people. And sharing our heritage is part of a recipe for a joyful soul. **It has always been my belief that the recipe of understanding one another's customs and cultures can help create a better relationship between Americans and people of foreign lands in the true meaning of world brotherhood.**

For that reason, as we break bread together, I bring to you the traditions and cultures of our people that exist here today as they did in the Land of my ancestors.

Some of the basic ingredients used in Middle Eastern foods.

Couscous grain; lemon; cilentro; anise seeds; burghul (fine cracked wheat #1 used for making tabooley); kishik (a mixture of yogurt and cracked wheat); pine nuts; chick peas, lentils; fava beans; burghul (coarse cracked wheat #3 for cooking); rice. Front row: whole nutmeg; allspice; za'tar; cardamon pods; sesame seeds; chick peas; black caraway seeds; parsley.

SPICES AND HERBS

Definitions - Arabic Translation

Spices and herbs exude an aroma that a gourmet appreciates as much as the taste. Taste and smell are so closely related that it is difficult to tell when aroma ends and flavor begins. There is a whiff of enticement about a sun-baked bed of herbs and their sweet aroma that are mindful of their Mediterranean heredity.

In Biblical times spices and herbs were the only known medicines. Caraway tea was sometimes used in the nursery to relieve colic, the seeds being a mild laxative. Coriander seed was an antidote against scorpion bites, and its incense was believed to expel evil spirits. Hippocrates praised mustard for its healing qualities. Today's mustard plaster dates back to the old treatments for respiratory ailments; even mustard-perfumed baths were said to help a cold. A sprig of anise was believed to ward off epilepsy, and an anise plant near the pillow of a bed was suppposed to restore youth and beauty. Anise is still used to treat throat irritations.

My kitchen contains all the spices and herbs used in these recipes. Keep in mind the old rule of all cooks; when in doubt, season to taste, but do not change the basic ingredients in the recipes.

Herbs are easy to grow, whether in window boxes, indoors in pots, or in a garden area. Most herbs need sun for at least four hours a day, while mint and parsely flourish in the shade. Some of the recipes call for mint, cilentro, parsley, thyme, bay leaf, caraway and marjoram.

Spices include all seasonings from the bark, root, stems, seeds, or fruit of aromatic plants and trees growing in tropical countries, Common spices used in Arabic cooking are allspice, cloves, nutmeg, cumin, ginger, saffron, and cinnamon, aniseed, sesame seeds and cardamon. Some aromatic seeds grow in America, but larger quantities are cultivated in Africa, Europe, South and Central America.

Preserving herbs. If you grow herbs in your garden, use them in fresh form. Otherwise, preserve them and use accordingly in these recipes. To preserve, pick off the tops and perfect leaves and scatter loosely in a tray. Put the tray in a dark, dry place. Drying should take from 3 to 4 days. When dry, crush the leaves and place in labeled jars.

MICRO-TIP: Take a large bunch of herbs, wrap loosely in paper towel and dry on high in your micro-wave for three to four minutes.

Baqdownis (Parsley) Rich in Vitamin C. For salads, soups, and garnishes.

Baqli (Purslane) Small plant with reddish stems, light green, tart fleshy leaves you can find growing wildly in your garden. Used in salads.

Bhar hub wa na'im (Allspice) Dried berry of pimento tree. Tastes like a combination of cloves, cinnamon, and nutmeg.

Hub-al-hal (Cardamon) An aromatic pod-shaped fruit with seeds inside. Used in Turkish coffee.

Hub-et il baraky (you're truly blessed with this black caraway seeds - baraky means to receive blessings) This biennial herb with aromatic fruit is known as caraway seed. Used in *talamee* (Syrian bun-type bread) and tasty in *Ka'ick* (Anise bread). Imported from Lebanon, Denmark, and Indonesia. A mild laxative. Added to tea, relieves the colic.

Junzabeel (Ginger) Zanziber plant grown in semi-tropical countries. Use whole in health drinks.

Kamoun (Cuminseed) Originally from Egypt. Slightly bitter flavor. Enhances the flavor of scrambled eggs. For indigestion, use 1 teaspoonful in powdered form, and follow with a glass of water. Annually exported by the ton from Turkey, Syria, and Iran. (**Matt. 23:23; Is. 28:25**)

Kizbara (Coriander, Cilentro) This flat-leaf parsley has a distinct flavor all of its own. These aromatic seeds are rich in Vitamin C. Used with meats and vegetables, especially with Fava Beans. (**Num. 11:7; Exod. 16-31**)

Mahleb (Black cherry kernels) Use in Syrian bun-type bread and Anise bread.

Mardakoosh (Marjoram) From the mint family. Aromatic and slightly bitter. Used in soups, salads, and meats.

Ma-war-id (Rose Water) and Mazaher (Orange blossom water) Flavor pastries, puddings and cakes. A must for a delicate *baklawa* syrup.

Na'na (Mint) A fragrant plant. Leaves, fresh or dried, flavor soups, meats, salads, and beverages. Spearmint is the variety most commonly grown. In gardens, it spreads abundantly. (**Matt. 23:23**)

Num-name or Hubaq (Basil, Sweet). Light yet spicy fragrance, basil can be used in salads, pestos, in fillings of boned lamb rolls. **In the year 313 A.D., St. Helena, mother of Roman Emperor Constantine made a pilgrimage to Jerusalem and was instrumental in finding the Cross upon which Jesus was crucifed. Surrounding the Cross was the basil plant. Highly revered in Orthodox churches, this plant adorns the Cross during processionals at Holy Week services.**

Simsum (Sesame Seed) Flavor pies, cookies, rolls and pastries. Sesame oil used for making *Baba Ghanouj and Tahini* sauce. Tons of this seed go into *halawa*, a mouth-watering Turkish candy.

Thume (garlic) From the lily family. For flavoring meats and salads (**Num. 11:5**)

Waraq al gar (bay leaf) Aromatic leaf of sweet bay or laurel tree. To flavor soups and meats. Historically, used as an antiseptic during epidemics, added to water for boiling of clothing.

<u>Yansoon</u> (Anise) Fruit of small annual plant which dries into the form of a seed. Used in Anise bread and Anise Tea. **(Matt. 23:23)**

<u>Za'tar</u> (Thyme) Pungent in taste. Dried, fresh, or chopped in salads, meat and poultry. Blend with sumac into powdered form and used in Lenten pies. Excellent on chicken smothered with *za' tar and sumac*.

Inviting guests over to enjoy a summer lunch
Cucumber Yogurt Salad, Grape Leaf Rolls, pocket bread filled with Yogurt Cheese Balls and mint, Baked Kibby, green beans, and rice.

ARABIC MENUS

The menus below are typical Arabic meals for each month of the year.

JANUARY DINNER MENU
Vegetable soup
Raw kibby
Cabbage rolls
Combination salad
Syrian bread
Coffee
Rice custard

FEBRUARY DINNER MENU
Kibby with yogurt-rice sauce
Meat pies
Fried cauliflower
Syrian bun-type bread
Coffee
Stuffed figs
Ricotta pastries

MARCH DINNER MENU
Eggplant stew
Spinach salad
Baked fish-*Tahini*
Coffee
Date crescents

APRIL DINNER MENU
   (Palm Sunday)
Shrimp cocktail
Assorted relishes
Baked stuffed fish
Baked eggplant
Sesame-oil with lemon
Lemon-Parsley salad
Turkish coffee
Turkish delight

MAY DINNER MENU
Marinated broiled chicken
Fried kibby
Wheat garden salad
Tabooley - Lettuce
Sun Tea

JUNE DINNER MENU
Raw Kibby
Roast chicken
Lamb-rice dressing
Syrian bread
Combination Salad
Stuffed shredded wheat

JULY DINNER MENU
(Have a Mansef Party) or
Baked kibby
Yogurt pies
Shish kebab
Corn on cob
Cucumber-yogurt salad
Sun tea
Fruit

AUGUST DINNER MENU
Stuffed grape leaves
Yogurt
Fava beans with lamb
Rice-orzo dressing
Beef tongue salad
Fruit and Coffee

SEPTEMBER DINNER MENU
Stuffed Squash
Fried kibby
Lamb liver
Beet salad
Turkish coffee

OCTOBER DINNER MENU
Lamb with Yogurt
Spinach Pies
Pickled Turnips
Mint tea
Almond rolls

NOVEMBER DINNER MENU
Pickled green peppers
Turkey
Rice-Giblet dressing
Stuffed grape leaves
Baked eggplant - Nut-filled cakes

DECEMBER DINNER MENU
Roast goose (rice-orzo in ring mold)
Baked kibby
Stuffed cabbage leaves
Spinach Salad
Diamond Pastry delights *Baklawa*

MEATLESS CHOICES

In photo: Cracked wheat with tomatoes; Fried cauliflower and Fried potatoes; Talamee and thin bread *marquq*; Steamed cauliflower and potatoes; Stewed eggplant *Imnazalee*; basket of vegetables squash, eggplant, tomatoes, garlic, onions; *Homos bi taheeni* with pocket bread; Pickled turnips; Chick Pea Soup.

Healthy Choices

Low-cholesterol Turkey Kibby (recipe, pg. 54)
Baked Kibby with Yogurt/nut mixture (recipe, pg. 54)
Pumpkin Kibby stuffed with spinach
(recipe, pg. 120)

Couscous topped with broiled vegetables
(recipe, pg. 50)

Falafel vegetable burger
(recipe, pg. 120)

Vegetarian pie - wreath garnish
(recipe, pg. 118)

APPETIZERS

Maza

When you enter a Middle Eastern home, it is obvious that the colorful appetizers produced are unexcelled in taste and artistry. There are from 20 to 50 countless varieties served as part of Arab hospitality's splendor. In every Syrian kitchen, *Sfeeha* (meat pies) and the national dish of Syria and Lebanon, *Kibby*, can be prepared in advance and stored in the freezer for unexpected guests and served as part of the *maza;* these miniature football-shaped *Kibby* are stuffed with lamb or beef and pine nuts, along with a *Kibby* stuffed with yogurt cheese, english walnuts and pomegranates. Sure to bring on raves is the tasty dip of eggplant, broiled and peeled, the pulp is mashed with *tahini*, garlic, and lemon and garnished with pine nuts and parsley.

Flat loaves of Arabic bread *khobaz* are used as scoops with the different spreads *Joban* and *Laban Dahareej* (cheeses), black olives glistening with olive oil, small pickled turnips that are pink from beets, *lahum nee* (raw lamb or beef) and *waraq inib mihshee* (grape leaves stuffed with chick peas, burghul and parsley) mellowed with lemon juice, are a few of the most popular appetizers served.

In **Egypt** *ful imdammas* is one of the national dishes enjoyed daily by millions; drizzled with lemon and olive oil, it is revered by rich and poor alike. Not only in Egypt, but all **Arabic** people relish the fava bean. (Mom's garden harvests the first fava bean plant as she makes sure to get her beans planted in early March).

From Janet David in Pennsylvania, Sadie Kanam of Canton, Ohio and Selma Johns Mesalem in Indianapolis, comes the best of *Shunkleesh*. Many of their familes migrated to Pennsylvania and other states from the county of *Hoson* in Syria where their *Shunkleesh* was in great demand. Attesting to this are the clergy who vie for their *Shunkleesh* as a conventioneer manages to slip this rare cheese to their favorite priest when noone is looking.

The maza dishes mentioned above can be found in the index. Here are a few samplings for any group or party.

RAW BEEF *Lahum nee* (known to the Western world as Steak Tartare)

1/2 pound round steak or sirloin, ground
1 large onion, chopped
1/2 teaspoon pepper
1/2 teaspoon salt
1/2 cup parsley or coriander
3 green onions, chopped fine

Knead all ingredients together. Serve as appetizer with Syrian bread. Goes well with anise-flavored liqueur *araq* also known as anisette. *Serves 3.*

SYRIAN CHEESE *Joban*
(cheese with junket)

1 gallon milk, homogenized or 2%
4 junket tablets

Have on hand colander and cheese cloth. Heat milk to lukewarm. Dissolve junket tablets in small amount of cool tap water. Add to milk. Mix with wooden spoon and set for 20 minutes. Stir with wooden spoon. Set for one hour or more. Cheese will settle on bottom. Pour into lined colander. Let set until all liquid is removed and cheese becomes solid. (If you need these immediately, cup your hands squeezing out moisture while you shape into rounds). Place in platter and sprinkle with salt. *Yield*: 5 *joban*, 5 inches in diameter, 1-1/2 inches thick.

COTTAGE CHEESE with LEMONS *Qareeshee ma' limoon*

1 quart liquid from Syrian Cheese
1 quart milk, 2% or 1-1/2%
Juice of 2 lemons

Heat liquid from Syrian Cheese on low fire until warm. Add milk. When milk rises, add lemon juice. Cook on low fire until cottage cheese gets thick. Pour into colander to strain off excess liquid. *Yield:* 2 cups.

YOGURT CHEESE *Labanee*

2 quarts yogurt mixed with
1/2 teaspoon salt

Pour yogurt in muslin or cheesecloth bag. Tie top of bag in knot and hang on kitchen sink faucet allowing excess liquid to go down the drain. Set overnight. Yogurt will become firm enough to use as a spread. Remove yogurt cheese following day and place in dish. Sprinkle with salt. Spread on flat loaves of Syrian bread for a delicious snack. *Yield:* 2-1/2 cups.

YOGURT BALLS *Laban dahareej* (Kids love this any time of the day spread on Syrian bread)

Yogurt Cheese   **Olive Oil**

Roll Yogurt Cheese into balls the size of golf balls. Place in a tray. Allow to set overnight in refrigerator until firm. Place in glass jar and cover with olive oil. Keep lid on jar. To serve, place in small dish and spoon small amount of oil over Yogurt Balls. Ready for your *maza* table when guests arrive. *Yield: 20.*

SPINACH FILLO TRIANGLES *Sabanegh ma' ajeen baklawa*

- 1 pound frozen chopped spinach thawed and drained well
- 1 small onion
- 1/4 cup olive oil
- 2 eggs
- 1 teaspoon salt
- 1/2 pound feta cheese, crumbled
- 1 teaspoon nutmeg
- 1/2 pound fillo pastry sheets
- 1 pound clarified butter, melted

FILLING: Thaw spinach in micro-wave oven. Squeeze out all moisture. Saute onion in olive oil; add spinach and salt. Cook on low heat for 5 minutes. Cool and add feta cheese. Mix in the eggs and nutmeg, blending all ingredients well.

Follow photo directions for Ricotta cheese pastries in preparing fillo flag-style, (pg. 100). Brush 3 sheets with butter and place a teaspoon filling at the edge of each triangle. Place on an ungreased baking tray. Fold flag-style brushing each fold with butter. Bake 20 minutes until golden. *Make these ahead and freeze. Bake frozen for 35 to 40 minutes in a 350º oven. Yield: approximately 70 triangles.*

SPINACH FETA IN FILLO DOUGH *Spanakopeta* (I've had many requests for this popular Greek recipe that I want to share with you.

- 2 pounds frozen spinach, chopped and drained
- 1 onion, chopped
- 4 tablespoons clarified butter
- 1 cup Cream Sauce*
- 6 eggs, beaten
- 1 cup crumbled feta cheese
- 1 teaspoon each salt and pepper
- Dash of nutmeg
- 1/2 pound fillo dough
- 1/2 pound clarified butter, melted

Saute onion in butter. Add spinach and saute 2 minutes. Cool. Mix in cream sauce, eggs, feta cheese, and seasonings. In an 11x14x2 inch pan, place 9 layers of fillo pastry sheets, brushing each with butter. Add the spinach-cheese mixture. Place 8 layers of fillo on top of filling, brushing each with butter. Sprinkle top layer lightly with cold water to prevent curling or breaking of fillo. Score top with a sharp knife in squares or diamond shape. Do not cut all the way through until after tray is baked. Bake in preheated 350º oven for 30 minutes, then place tray on top rack of oven and continue baking another 10 minutes until crust is a golden shade. Yield: 16 squares.

*Cream Sauce: Melt 2 tablespoons butter in pan, add 1-1/2 tablespoons flour. Gradually stir in milk. Continue cooking, stirring on medium fire until sauce is thick and smooth. Stir in 1/2 teaspoon salt and dash of white pepper. Cover until ready to use. Yield: 2 cups.

Shunkleesh from Janet David of Pennsylvania

5 pounds dry cottage cheese **1/2 cup salt**

Mix cheese and salt together until very smooth. Drain in colander lined with cheesecloth. Place colander over bowl to let water drain from cheese for approximately 2 to 3 days. Put cheese in another bowl and mix with hands until smooth. Roll balls size a of baseball.

Dry cheese balls on white cloth for 4 days, changing cloth when wet to keep cheese dry. When dry, put each ball in a small plastic sandwich bag and then in a container with lid. Check after a month to see if mold forms. After they are moldy, wrap in nylon net and wash off all the mold under running cold water. Dry the balls and roll in a small amount of olive oil and then in oregano. Place back in container for a few days. *Serve with scrambled eggs or as an appetizer with Syrian bread. Yield: 7 or 8.*

TAHINI - *Taratoor*

1 cup tahini **2 cloves garlic, crushed with salt**
4 tablespoons water **2 tablespoons parsley, chopped**
Juice of 3 lemons **1/4 cup pine nuts, sauteed lightly**

Pour 1 cup *tahini* in blender or food processor. Puree about 5 to 10 seconds until smooth. Add water and lemon juice and blend into a smooth sauce. Mix in crushed garlic. Serve on an oval platter. If you refrigerate before garnishing, it will get thick. Just add more water to desired consistency. Garnish with parsley and pine nuts. Paprika adds a nice color as a garnish. *Serves 6.*

CHICK-PEA *Tahini* Dip *Homos bi Tahini*

1 cup *tahini* (prepare recipe above) **1 tablespoon olive oil**
2 cups chick peas, fresh or canned **1/2 teaspoon salt**
1/2 teaspoon baking soda **3 tablespoons chopped parsley**
1/4 cup chick pea liquid

Soak chick peas with baking soda in cold water overnight. Following day drain off water. Place peas in kettle, add water to cover; cook in covered kettle until well done, about 45 minutes. (Soaking is not necessary if using canned chick peas). Reserve 1/4 cup chick pea liquid. Using processor or blender, process the chick peas with the liquid. Add *tahini* (see preceding recipe) and salt and process until smooth. Place in a flat oval dish. Make several dents in mixture and spoon olive oil into dents. Garnish with parsley and pine nuts. *(If pomegranates are in season, these tasty seeds make a pretty garnish) Serves 6.*

EGGPLANT with *Tahini Baba Ghanouj*

1 medium eggplant, dark skinned
2 cloves garlic
1 teaspoon salt
3 tablespoons *tahini*
Juice of 2 lemons
2 tablespoons water
2 tablespoons each of pine nuts, pomegranate seeds and chopped parsley

Pierce eggplant with fork to let steam escape. Broil with skin on, turning it frequently. Remove skin under cold water and mash the pulp. Pound garlic with salt, add *tahini*, lemon juice, and water. Then mix with eggplant and salt. Spread on a platter and garnish with pine nuts, pomegranate seeds and parsley. *Serves 4.* Line platter with *zatar chips*.

EGGPLANT with LABAN *Batinjan imfasakh*

2 large eggplants
1/4 cup olive oil
1 cup yogurt
1 teaspoon salt
1 clove garlic

Skin eggplants. Slice very thin. Sprinkle small amount of salt on slices to drain off excess moisture. (This will prevent eggplant from absorbing too much oil when fried). Fry in oil until golden brown. Remove from oil and mash. Add yogurt and mix well. Crush garlic and add to mixture. *Yield:* 4 cups.

ZA'TAR CHIPS *Try these crispy chips at your next party with baba-ghanouj*

4 loaves pocket bread (pita)
1/2 cup za'tar
1/2 cup olive oil

Split pocket bread in half and tear in pieces. Mix *za'tar* and oil. Coat bread lightly with mixture. Broil 30 seconds until toasted. *These will go fast, so make enough for munching all evening.*

AVOCADO with *Tahini* (add 1 pound of cooked shrimp if you like)

1 ripe avocado, mashed
3 tablespoons *tahini*
Juice of 2 lemons
2 tablespoons water
1 clove garlic
Salt and pepper to taste

Mash avocado and add to *tahini* with lemon juice. Blend until mixture is smooth. Add garlic, water and seasonings. Spread on crackers. An added treat: Cook 1 pound shrimp, chop and mix in with avocado mixture. Serve with pocket bread wedges.

BEEF TONGUE with TAHINI (prepare beef tongue page 33). Slice tongue and top with tahini sauce. Excellent appetizer served with pocket bread wedges.

TAHINI with LABAN *Imtabil*

In food processor, mix together **1 cup tahini and 1 cup yogurt.** Crush **1 clove garlic** with salt and add to mixture. Garnish with chopped parsley and sauteed pine nuts. *Serves 4.*

This quotation by Daniel Webster is embedded on the walls of the Senate corridors, Capitol Bldg., Washington, D.C..

My grandparents and parents were farmers in Syria. (pg. 51) I am blessed with a heritage that brought this knowledge with them when they migrated to America. Our cupboards are always filled with **high fibre grains** that have always been man's first source of nutrition along with a myriad of other staples used in what is **known as today's nutritional 'health-watch'.**

These are staples that have been available since biblical times. My pantry and freezer are filled with rice, orzo, lentils, lima beans, green beans, fava beans, couscous, falafel, chick peas, burghul, barley, pasta, pine nuts, almonds, tahini, and along with these healthy foods, we always exercised. Planting a garden and fruit trees, raking leaves and taking long walks promises to keep the pounds off.

A profound Arabic saying: **"He who denies his heritage has no heritage"**. *"Halee byin-kor asloo, ma 'indoo asal"*.

*Helen's maternal grandfather
Boutros Samaan
(former Mayor of Arne, Syria) Sheikh il Balad*

This is my heritage and in retrospect I look back in history to my grandparents and thank them for teaching future generations this healthy way of life.

THE WONDERFUL WORLD OF YOGURT

SYRIA AND LEBANON *Laban* - **TURKEY** *Yoghurta*
EGYPT *Laban zabady* - **ARMENIA** *Madzoon*

The Bible frequently refers to it as a healthful and filling food. **Laban** has been used for the treatment of burns and cuts and a dietetic for stomach ulcers and a myriad of intestinal disorders. Nobel Peace prize winner Ilya Metchnikoff, the Russian bacteriologist who headed the Pastuer Institute in Paris discovered yogurt produced friendly bacteria (bacillus bulgaricus) and it worked like an antibiotic. Since then there have been many theories on the miracles of yogurt. Longevity has been contributed to consuming this on a daily basis. An important part of the Middle Eastern diet, there isn't a day that goes by without *laban* on our table. A special treat for children is *'aroos labanee* yogurt, removed of whey, becomes a creamy cheese spread on *marquq,* a flat Syrian bread that's rolled up and enhanced by adding fresh mint and green onions. The Bible refers to *laban* as a precious asset of the Land of Promise, since it flowed, not with milk and honey as in the English translation, but with *laban* and honey.

While *laban* was made centuries ago from the milk of goats and sheep, today it is made mostly from cow's milk; 2% or 1% and skim milk. I've tried them all and they will produce creamy *laban,* the texture and thickness of pudding.

Middle Eastern people do not restrict the use of *Laban.* It enhances the tastes of many foods. We use it as an accompaniment to rice and cracked wheat dishes, rolled grape leaves and especially with *imjaddara,* a healthy lentil-wheat dish. It is excellent served with little meat pies *Sfeeha* that Syrian cooks bake by the dozens. And the sauces are fragrant and delectable, especially a gourmet's delight is *koosa ablama*, a summer squash stuffed with pine nuts and minced lamb and cooked in a yogurt sauce sprinkled with dry mint. On a cold winter day our friends can't wait until they come over for some *Kibby labaneeyee* cooked in a rice-yogurt sauce.

THE MAKING OF LABAN is the simplist of culinary arts; but there is a certain knack of making it perfect. The success or failure of *laban* is usually dependent on having the right temperature. It should be warm enough for the yogurt germ to spread. Once you've learned the procedure of the right temperature via the finger test, you'll find yourself making *laban* daily.

LABAN (this is a simple recipe heating the milk in the micro-wave oven)

1 gallon milk, 2%, homogenized or skim
4 heaping tablespoons yogurt starter *rowbee* kept on hand from a previous batch of yogurt or use commercial plain yogurt (My preference is Dannon's labeled with it's live culture)

Have on hand a heavy bath towel - a blanket will work well also
Lid for covering container

Place milk in a micro-wave bowl. Cook on high for 30 minutes until it poaches on top. Remove from micro-wave and set on towel. It should take about 45 minutes to cool to 110° temperature. However, it is not necessary to use a thermometer. Immerse your little finger in the milk to the count of 10. If you can't keep the finger in to the count of 10, the milk is too hot; and if you can keep it in longer than the count of 10, the milk is too cold and you should reheat it.

In a small bowl, mix the 4 tablespoons of yogurt starter with a little of the hot milk until it is smooth and creamy. Pour it into the hot milk, stirring well with a wooden spoon. Cover with lid and wrap securely with the towel or blanket to preserve heat. Store in warm place for 6 hours. Remove lid. After a few minutes, refrigerate. When it cools, the yogurt will jell like pudding and depending on the starter, will taste sweet or tart.

If using starter from yogurt that has been under refrigeration for a week or more, the results will be tart or sharp. (This is best for making sauces). If the starter is from fresh yogurt only a few days old, the taste will be sweeter.

FOR A THICK YOGURT: When it completely cools, cover yogurt with white paper towel, placing a white terry towel on top of paper towel to absorb any excess whey. Continue to wring out excess whey as often as you like if you want an extremely thick yogurt. **However, if you plan to make sauces, DO NOT wring out whey.**

Once you've accomplished making your first batch of yogurt, you'll find yourself making a gallon a week and reaping the healthy benefits it offers. If you think a gallon is more than you want on hand, keep in mind the other uses that these various chapters offer. Under the Appetizer chapter, you'll want to make Yogurt Cheese and then you can preserve extra *labanee* to have on hand for an instant snack. You can also freeze the Yogurt Cheese to have on hand for making some *Fatayer Laban.* These disappear as fast as you can make them.

NOTE: Most cooks have a micro-wave oven in their kitchen. However, in the event you do not have one and want to make it the traditional way, follow this method. Heat milk in a saucepan on low fire until it comes to a boil and poaches on top, about 30 minutes. Pour into another bowl and proceed with above directions of cooling down. (One of the nice things about using a micro-wave container, there is no need to transfer to another bowl, and no more scrubbing of milk from bottom of pan). And you can make smaller amounts. For **1/2 gallon milk, use 3 heaping tablespoons of yogurt starter** and cook in microwave for 20 minutes. Let set about 30 minutes for the cool down period to 110°. Follow procedure above.

KISHIK

This blend of *laban and burghul* (cracked wheat), is dried for many days under the sun, then run through a sieve until it is a fine dry powder. But with today's methods of using food processors I had success making my own *kishik.**

Use 1-1/2 quarts tart *laban* at least a week old. (It must be tart to produce a good *kishik)* Do not remove the whey from the laban. It should be liquidy to absorb into the wheat.

4 cups cracked wheat #2 grain*

Blend together the above ingredients with your hands, mixing well. Place in a container with a lid. Repeat the mixing as though you were kneading dough for at least 15 days or more. The mixture will swell and get foamy when it is ready. You'll get a whiff of *kishik* when that happens.

Place a table outdoors with a clean white sheet on it. Make sure it is a very sunny day and the air is dry. Spread the *kishik* on the cloth, about pea size or smaller, rubbing it as you spread. Cover with a screen.* During the day, rub the *kishik* moving it around the cloth so that all sides will become completely dry. This will take a full day under the sun. Place in food processor and process as fine as possible and you'll reward yourself with 6 cups of *kishik*.

Please note: The *kishik* that you purchase from a store will be of a corn meal texture. The *kishik* from this recipe may turn out a little coarser, but the end result is the same. (I couldn't wait to make my *kibby kishik* as soon as it was ready).

**Kishik* and cracked wheat may be purchased at Middle Eastern specialty shops. Purchase screen from any hardware store.

Kibby Kishik

A note about
Chicken Rice Soup *Shouraba il roz*
(aka **Helen's Proven Cure-all Soup***) on page 11:*

Helen prepared this soup for a guest bishop to St. George Orthodox Church in Indianapolis. He was to speak to a ladies' luncheon at noon and a banquet the same evening. A bout of the flu forced him to cancel his luncheon engagement. Helen asked the parish priest if she could make him this soup for his evening meal, to which the priest replied, "Yes, and make enough for all the clergy!" She immediately sent out for five chickens to be prepared in the church kitchen. The next morning during the Divine Liturgy, the bishop announced, "I wouldn't be here today if it had not been for Helen Corey's Cure-all Chicken Soup, which cured me overnight!"

And that was not the only time she has prepared this soup for those stricken with the flu or a cold. It has been featured over the years in a number of magazines.

SOUPS

Shouraba

Soups have an international appeal. As with wine, aging improves the flavor; soup dishes are usually better the second day. In the Middle East, soups do not usually form part of the menu when there is a multitude of cereal, meat and vegetable dishes from which to choose. However, on cold winter days, soup is prepared as the principal dish of the meal. Some of the most popular soups are *Mlukheeyeh*, a national dish of **Egypt;** the soothing tasty Chicken-rice soup of **Syria** helps cure colds and the flu; another favorite is Lentils and wheat with *kishik* ; and a popular soup in **Lebanon** is *Imjadarra Humra..*

CHICKEN RICE SOUP *Shouraba il roz*

1 - 4 pound fryer, sectioned for cooking **Salt and pepper to taste**
1 cup chopped celery **1/2 cup rice**
Dash of each, allspice and cinnamon

Simmer chicken, covered, in water until tender. Skim off scum from surface. When cool, debone. Add chicken back to pot, along with celery, spice, and seasoning. When celery is almost tender (about 15 minutes) add Minute˙ rice and cook another 15 minutes. *Serves 6–7.*

CHICK PEA SOUP *Shouraba il homos*

2 cups chick peas, dry **1/2 cup olive oil**
1 teaspoon baking soda **2 large onions, chopped**
1/2 teaspoon salt **1/2 teaspoon each of salt and pepper**

Soak peas overnight in baking soda and salt. Following day rinse well and rub peas between fingers to remove skins. Rinse again, cover with water, and simmer until tender. Add remaining ingredients and cook until done, about 30 minutes. *Serves 4.*

LENTILS AND WHEAT WITH KISHIK *Imjadara mar-qoo-a*

2 cups Lentils and Wheat **2 tablespoons butter**
   (see Lenten section) **1 cup *kishik***
1 onion, minced **2 cups water**

Saute onion in butter. Add *kishik* and mix well. Add water and stir. Add 2 cups Lentils and Wheat and continue stirring for 2 minutes over medium fire. *Serves 4.*

LENTIL AND WHEAT SOUP *Imjadara Humra*

 2 cups lentils
 10 cups water
 4 onions, julienned
 3/4 cup olive oil
 2 cups cracked wheat
 1-1/2 tablespoons salt

Sort and rinse lentils in water. Cover lentils with 10 cups water. Boil 30 minutes. While lentils are cooking, fry onions in oil until a very rich brown. Set to one side. Add cracked wheat to lentils and boil on a medium fire. Add salt and oil that onions were cooked in. Cover and simmer for 1 hour. Take the crispy dry browned onions and crush to a paste. Garnish the finished soup with the onions and lemon wedges. *Serves 8.* Onions really enhance this dish... the more the better!

KISHIK SOUP

 1/4 cup oil
 1 onion, chopped
 1 cup *kishik*
 3 cups water

Saute onion in oil until soft. Mix with *kishik* and simmer for 1 minute. Add water. Stir and cook for 5 minutes until thick. This a very nourishing and filling soup. *Serves 4.*

VEGETABLE SOUP *Shouraba il khuthra*

 1 pound shin beef with bones
 3-1/2 quarts cold water
 2 tablespoons salt
 1 clove garlic, minced
 1/2 cup minced onion
 3/4 cup diced celery
 2 cups shredded green cabbage
 1 cup diced carrots
 1 No. 2 can tomatoes
 1/8 teaspoon pepper
 4 tablespoons minced parsley

Combine beef, water, and salt. Cover and bring to a boil. Skim. Cover and simmer 1 hour. Remove bone. Add remaining ingredients, except parsley. Cover and simmer 30 minutes. Sprinkle with parsley and serve. *Serves 8.*

BARLEY SOUP *Hareesee - Qamheeyee (John 6:9, 13)*

 1 pound pearl barley (*qameh maqshoor*)
  or peeled wheat
 2 pounds chicken parts (or 2 pounds lamb chunks)
 1 gallon water
 1 tablespoon salt
 1 teaspoon pepper

Soak barley for 12 hours. (If other than pearl barley is used soak for 1 hour.)

In deep pot, add barley to chicken parts (or lamb). Cover with 1 gallon water. Bring to a boil. Skim foam on top. When broth is clear, add salt and pepper. Cover and simmer approximately one hour until poultry or meat is fork tender. Remove poultry from pot. Cool and strain so that all bones are removed from chicken. Return chicken pieces to the pot. Stir often until soup thickens. *Serves 8.*

YOGURT-CUCUMBER SOUP   (A cool refreshing summer soup)
Shouraba khyar ma' laban

2 tablespoons butter
1 small onion, finely chopped
1 small garlic clove, minced
2 cucumbers, peeled and sliced thin
2 tablespoons flour
2 cups chicken stock
2 cups plain yogurt
1 teaspoon salt
1/2 teaspoon white pepper
8 thin slices of cucumber with peel on for garnish

In large skillet melt butter. Add onion and garlic and saute until soft. Add cucumber slices and cook slowly until soft. Remove from heat. Stir in flour. Blend in chicken stock, stirring well. Place in 2 quart pan and cook over medium heat, bringing to a boil. Reduce heat and simmer 5 minutes. Remove from heat and place one cup at a time in processor and puree. Pour in serving bowl. Cover and chill. Before serving, add yogurt and stir well. Add seasonings. Garnish with thin slices of cucumbers. *Serves 4.*

---

*EGYPTIANS with their ancient monuments of the Pyraminds and the Sphynx, their Mamluk mosques, and the citadel of Muhammad Ali - modern Egypt is just as much a gift of the Nile as it was when Herodotus first coined the phrase. (The Egyptians diet ingredients of melons, legumes, pomegranates, dates, fish from the river and sea and an abundant variety of herbs and spices are recorded in ancient wall paintings in the tombs of the Pharoahs). Ancient Egyptians are believed to have been the first people to make leavened bread. Actual examples of bread made 4,000 years ago have been found in sealed tombs. One of the main suppliers of wheat and barley to Rome, and wild barley is still found on the shores of the Red Sea where it was originally discovered by the goddess Isis.

The onion and the closely related garlic and leek families, had an almost religious significance in ancient Egypt. Wall paintings show priests holding up bunches of onions; papyrus texts tell of special days for tying onions around the throat or stomach, and a day for walking with onions in processions. To this day, on the eve of Sham an-Nassim, Egyptians put a piece of green onion or garlic under their pillows and the next morning crush and smell it before going out to "sniff the breezes" on the first day of spring.

Egypt's true national dish - and eaten and known as Egyptian throughout the Middle East is *mlukheeyeh*. This is made from a spinach-like pot herb, <u>Corchorus olitorius</u> (Jews's mallow, according to Webster's). The leaves are cut and recut until they become almost a green paste. A few minutes of boiling turns the dish a blackish green, ready to be ladled over plates of rice, pieces of dried bread and chicken, lamb or young rabbit. *Aramco World Magazine, November-December, 1975.*

MLUKHEEYEH, a superb culinary experience (Men like this dish particularly with lots of garlic. Riyad Bannourah can't wait to go home and eat his wife Hala's version of this dish that has created poetic praise from many)

- 1 fryer, 4 pound, skinned and sectioned for cooking
- 1/4 cup lemon juice mixed with 1/4 cup vinegar
- 1 tablespoon salt
- 1/2 cup butter or margarine
- 1/2 pound mlukheeyeh, crushed
- 3 cloves garlic
- 8 cups water
- 1 large onion
- 1 tablespoon salt
- 1 teaspoon allspice
- 2 tablespoon butter

Marinate the skinned chicken pieces in lemon juice, vinegar and salt for 1 hour. While chicken is marinating, saute the garlic and crushed *mlukheeyeh* in 1/2 cup butter until all butter is absorbed. Remove the chicken from marinade. Place chicken pieces in kettle filled with 8 cups of water. (Add more if you desire a thinner soup). Add onion, salt and allspice, cover and cook for 35 minutes. When the chicken is half-way cooked, add lemon juice and the *mlukheeyeh..* Cover the kettle and cook on low heat until it thickens, about 35 minutes. Saute 3 more cloves of garlic in 2 tablespoons butter and add to the pot. *Serves 6-8.* (Lamb is also an excellent addition along with the chicken - just cook the lamb cubes until tender and add along with the strained broth to the above).

PASSOVER: Historical origin: EXODUS 13, verses 3, 33, 34, 39, 42, 43.

CHICKEN SOUP AND MATZO BALLS (Served during Passover Meals in Jewish homes)

SOUP: (This recipe comes from Louise Sommers with praises from husband Walter)

- 2 - 3 to 4 pound fryers
- 1/2 teaspoon each salt, pepper, Lawry's seasoned salt and poultry seasoning
- 1 onion
- 2 carrots, sliced
- 2 stalks celery
- 4 sprigs parsley

Clean the chickens and rub seasonings over all. Place in large pot and cover with water reaching at least two inches over chickens. Cook until chickens are tender. Remove chickens and set aside for other chicken dishes. Only the broth is used for the soup. Strain the chicken soup and set in refrigerator overnight. Following day, lift off fat and discard. If you desire additional flavor, add Croyden House' Instant Soup Mix.

MATZO BALLS:
   Mix together; 1/2 stick Fleischmann's salt-free margarine, room temperature
   4 eggs, room temperature

   Mix in 5/8 cup Matzo meal. Add dash of nutmeg and salt. Refrigerate overnight.

   Form mixture into small balls. Boil the soup. Drop matzo balls into the soup. Cook covered at medium heat for one hour.

Rabbi Joseph P. Klein, United Hebrew Congregation, Terre Haute, Indiana shared the following explanation of festivals as they appear in **Leviticus 23**. (There are 6 major festivals - these are a few.)

"SHABBAT / SABBATH:" The Sabbath is welcomed into one's home as part of the Sabbath evening meal. After lighting and blessing two candles, the family recites/sings the blessing over, and then drinks wine as the symbol of (Sabbath) joy. The wine is customarily red and sweet, so that with its smell, sight and taste it reminds us of the sparkling sweetness of our Sabbath joy. Following the blessing over bread, the family cuts or breaks the Sabbath challah, a sweet, heavy and braided bread. Traditionally there are two loaves of challah on the table, representing the double portion of manna the Isrealites collected on Friday (**Ex. 16:5**).

With these three blessings, the Sabbath has begun and the meal is served. While there is no customary or traditional meal, many American families begin with chicken or matzo-ball soup. The main course will vary with family traditions."

"The Pilgrimage Festivals" *"PESACH/PASSOVER*

The week-long Passover observance is focused on the absence of leavened foods. Though it is not so observed in Bible times, since the 2nd Century BCE, Jewish families have celebrated the first (and often the second night as well) of Passover with a Seder Service. The Seder (Hebrew for "order") retells the story of the exodus from Egypt, using foods as a symbolic means, a reminder of the pain of slavery and the joy of freedom. In addition to the removal of all unleavened products from the house, traditional families will also use separate Passover plates and cooking utensils throughout the week."

"The 'High Holidays' ROSH/HASHANA/NEW YEAR

Called in Leviticus a convocation announced with trumpets, this special sabbath (rest day) was called 'Rosh Hashana'. Representing the hope for a sweet year, families begin their meal with apples and honey, and 'break bread' with a circular challah, symbolic of the renewal of the calendar cycle. The meal is festive and full of expectation that the new year will bring blessing and health, happiness and joy."

A maza plate of Baba Ghanouj with Zatar chips

Healthy Lentils and Cracked wheat garnished with an onion flower

Appetizing health salad Tabooley fill tomato cups and peppers

SALADS

Salata

One of the most popular salads in Syria and Lebanon is *Tabooley*, also known as *Suf*. It's an absolute must for me to have tomatoes, green onions, mint and lettuce in my garden for my *Tabooley* parties. Some of our most popular parties took place under our grapevine arbor. Reaching up for a grape leaf, utensils are put to one side as the leaf is used to scoop up the salad and deftly place it in the mouth. Stuffing tomato cups with *tabooley* is a most colorful party salad that will bring on raves.

You're sure to be asked for the recipe when you serve the tasty spinach salad sprinkled with the sweet-tasting pomegranate seeds. The pomegranate is widely cultivated in **Palestine** and throughout **Syria**. Its cultivation encircled the Mediterranean and extended through **Arabia** long ago. This fruit grows on a shrub. The rind is thick and red with a bright yellow hue on the inside. It is filled with a large number of red seeds, consisting of a delicate juice. The seeds are separated by a delicate white membrane. One must take care in breaking open this fruit so that the juice will not squirt on your clothes. (It will stain). It makes a wonderful garnish for many poultry and fish dishes as well as a garnish for salads.

An origin of the Middle East and now featured in many American restaurants is the healthy yogurt-cucumber salad. We top it with a hint of crushed mint with its fragrance permeating in the many delectable dishes found herein.

A wild plant that is a favorite of Middle Eastern people is *jirjeeree (watercress)*. Our friends get together a carload of watercress seekers and drive off to the nearest stream or brook to pluck them out of the water. They're so tasty eaten raw that it's difficult to keep from eating them on the way home. When we lived in Canton, Ohio, all the relatives took carloads to get their *jirjeeree* from streams at Monument Park, not too far from where the present Hall of Fame now stands. In many communities where Middle Eastern people live, there are special places to find this rarety, but very few will reveal the location for fear there will be a surge of seekers and the watercress will disappear.

What appears to be weeds to some people, is food on the table for the knowledgable, and an excellent source of vitamins. First to be found in the spring is the dandelion. Mom and I go out to fields that haven't been treated by chemicals, carrying our paper sacks and knives, we dig away at the young tender dandelion greens before the blossoms appear. Loaded with Vitamin A, eaten in salads, cooked or raw, this nutritious dandelion is delicious with a spread of yogurt cheese in *kmaj* Arabic bread sandwiches. It is important to wash the greens thoroughly, changing the water at least four or five times. Let them soak awhile, making them even more tender and removing any bitterness that might exist.

WHEAT GARDEN SALAD *Tabooley or Suf* EVERYONE's FAVORITE

1 cup cracked wheat, fine grain	4 large tomatoes
1 bunch green onions	Juice of 4 lemons
2 large bunches parsley	1/4 cup olive oil
2/3 cup fresh mint leaves	1 teaspoon salt
(or 1/2 cup dried mint)	1/2 teaspoon pepper

Rinse wheat in water until no longer cloudy. Soak for 5 minutes. Squeeze dry by cupping hands and pressing between palms of hands. Use food processor to pulsate parsley to save time (or chop fine on your cutting board) Chop onions, mint leaves and tomatoes very fine. Place vegetables in large bowl; add wheat, lemon juice, oil, salt and pepper and mix well. Serve with fresh grape or lettuce leaves used as scoops. *Serves 6.*

WHEAT GARDEN SALAD **PARTY SERVING FOR 125**

6 cups cracked wheat, fine grain	10 pounds tomatoes
14 bunches parsley	2 cups lemon juice
2 bunches mint	3 cups olive or salad oil
10 bunches green onions	Salt and pepper to taste

Use same procedure as above. If you have a processor, shorten preparation time by processing the parsley. *Serves 125.*

PURSLANE SALAD *Salata Buqli - Farfaheeni*

In looking for this in your lawn area, this is a green leafy plant with a touch of raspberry color on the inside of the leaf. The leaves are thick, crispy and have a tasty lemony flavor. Pluck them for a salad only if your lawn is not treated with chemicals.

1 pound purslane	2 tablespoon olive oil
1 medium onion, chopped	salt and pepper to taste
3 tablespoons lemon juice	

Mix together above ingredients. *Serves 4.*

SPINACH SALAD WITH POMEGRANATE SEEDS *Salata Sabanigh ma' raman*

> 1 pound fresh spinach
> 1 medium onion
> 2 tomatoes, sliced in eighths
> 1/2 cup english walnuts, chopped
> 1 teaspoon salt
> 1/2 teaspoon pepper
> 2 tablespoons lemon juice
> 1-1/2 tablespoons olive oil
> 1/4 cup pomegranate seeds

Chop the spinach. Peel, slice and add onion. Add the tomatoes, 1/2 cup english walnuts, salt and pepper. Toss lightly. Drizzle lemon juice and olive oil to coat salad. Toss again. Garnish with pomegranate seeds. *Serves 4*. (A colorful salad to serve with your Christmas meal.) Your guests will ask for seconds. Double the ingredients to serve 8.

WATERCRESS SALAD *Salata jirjeeree*

> 1/3 cup olive oil
> 1 large clove garlic, chopped
> 1/3 cup pine nuts
> 1 pound watercress, rinsed well and chopped
> 1 large onion, chopped
> 2 tablespoons lemon juice
> Salt and pepper to taste

Heat olive oil in skillet. Add garlic and cook until brown. Remove and discard garlic. Add pine nuts and saute until golden. Remove from skillet. Remove moisture from watercress. Place the chopped watercress in a bowl, mix in onions, and drizzle on the lemon juice and oil from skillet. Toss, then sprinkle on pine nuts for garnish. *Serves 4*. (Or if you prefer, mound fresh and crisp watercress on platter and serve with your meal) Tasty without any condiments.

BEEF TONGUE SALAD *Salata il sane*

> 1 small beef tongue, cooked (see Index)
> 1 onion, chopped
> Juice of 1 lemon
> 6 sprigs of parsley, chopped
> Salt and pepper to taste
> 1/2 teaspoon garlic powder
> 1/8 cup olive oil

Slice and cube tongue. Add remaining ingredients and toss. *Serves 4*.

LEMON PARSLEY WALNUT SALAD *Salata baqdownis ma' limoon*

> 2 lemons
> 3 bunches flat-leaf parsley, chopped fine
> 1 small onion, chopped
> 1 cup walnuts, ground in food processor until moist and crumbly
> 1/2 cup olive oil
> Salt and pepper to taste

Peel and seed the lemons. Then mince them on cutting board (or pulsate on food processor) until pulpy. Place in large mixing bowl and add remaining ingredients. Mix everything together until well blended. Serve with *lahum mishwee (shish kebab)*. This salad is a refreshing change from other salads with it's lemony taste. I serve it often to guests. (Thanks to Ma'moun and Julie Sukkar for this Damascus recipe)

DANDELION SALAD *Salata hindbee*

(The name is believed to have originated from the likeness of the leaves to a lion's tooth.) Be sure to soak the leaves thoroughly to remove bitterness.

- 1 pound dandelion greens
- 1 large onion
- Juice of 2 lemons
- 1/4 cup olive oil
- 1/2 teaspoon garlic powder
- Salt and pepper to taste

Chop dandelion greens and onions. Add lemon juice, oil and seasonings. Mix well and serve. *Serves 4.*

BEET SALAD *Salata il shamunder*

- 3 large cooked beets, diced
- 1 onion, minced
- 2 tablespoons chopped parsley
- Salt and pepper to taste
- 1/8 cup olive oil
- 2 tablespoons wine vinegar

Combine beets with onion, parsley, salt and pepper. Coat salad with oil and vinegar. Chill and serve. *Serves 4-6.*

CUCUMBER-YOGURT SALAD *Khyar ma' laban*

- 1 large cucumber, peeled and diced
- 1 clove garlic or 1/2 teaspoon garlic powder
- 1/2 teaspoon salt
- 1 quart yogurt
- 1 tablespoon dried mint

Mash garlic with salt and add to yogurt. Add diced cucumber to yogurt. Garnish with dried mint. *Serves 4.* (Try this for lunch - Arabic pocket bread filled with cucumber-yogurt)

EGGPLANT SALAD *Salata il batinjan*

    2 large eggplants, pierced with fork   **1/2 cup olive oil**
    3 tomatoes, quartered   **3 tablespoons wine vinegar**
    1 small onion, diced   **Salt and pepper to taste**
    2 tablespoons chopped parsley

Bake eggplants in moderate oven (350°) for 45 minutes. Remove, dip in cold water and peel. Rub salad bowl with garlic and place diced eggplant in bowl. Add rest of ingredients and marinate one hour before serving. *Serves 6.*

LENTIL SALAD *Salata addis*

    1/2 pound brown lentils   **1 small chopped onion**
    3-1/2 cups water   **2 tablespoons chopped parsley**
    1 bay leaf   **1 tomato, diced**
    1 clove garlic, crushed   **1 tablespoon lemon juice**
    1 small onion   **3 tablespoons olive oil**
    Salt and pepper to taste

Sort and rinse lentils. Drain and place in saucepan. Add water, bay leaf, onion, salt and pepper. Bring to a boil and cook partly covered about 30 minutes. Discard the onion and bay leaf, and drain the lentils. In a mixing bowl, add lentils to chopped onions, parsley, garlic, tomatoes, lemon, oil, and seasonings. *Serves 4.*

There is nothing as satisfying as *Salata Khuthra*, the Syrian combination salad, with its olive oil trickling over all the vegetables and flavored with fragrant mint. The secret of this tasty salad lies in the expert handling of the seasonings. Most Middle-Eastern people make this salad at a moment's notice by reaching out to their gardens where they grow an abundance of vegetables.

COMBINATION SALAD *Salata khuthra*

    3 tomatoes   2 tablespoons fresh or dried mint
    1/2 bunch green onions   6 radishes
    1 green pepper   1 teaspoon garlic powder
    1 avocado (optional)   Salt and pepper to taste
    1 head of lettuce (optional)   1/4 cup olive oil
    1/2 bunch parsley   Juice of 2 lemons

Chop vegetables and combine. Add seasonings, olive oil and lemon juice; toss and serve. *Serves 8.*

In **Syria, Palestine, Jordan** and especially **in Egypt**, *Ful imdamis,* made with a dried broad bean also known as fava beans, is in great demand. Most Egyptians begin their day with this seasoned bean for breakfast. **(Ez. 4:9)**

FAVA BEAN SALAD *Ful imdamis*

- 1 teaspoon baking soda
- 2 cups dried fava beans
- 1 onion, chopped
- 1 clove garlic, chopped
- 2 tomatoes, chopped
- 6 sprigs finely chopped parsley
- 2 tablespoons lemon juice
- 1-1/2 tablespoons olive oil

Soak beans overnight in water with baking soda. Following day rinse; cover with fresh water and boil for 1 hour. Cool, then add onion, garlic, tomatoes, parsley, lemon juice and oil. *Serves 4*. NOTE; Fava beans can be purchased by the pound at Middle Eastern stores listed in Shoppers' Guide. Canned fava beans are available. If using canned beans, just add the vegetables and dressing above.

LIMA BEAN SALAD *Salata fasoolya*

- 1/2 pound lima beans
- 1 teaspoon salt
- 1 clove garlic, minced
- Juice of 1 lemon
- 2 tablespoons olive oil

Boil beans until tender and drain. Add salt, garlic, lemon juice and oil to beans. Mix thoroughly. Serve hot or cold. *Serves 3*. NOTE: String beans may be substituted for limas.

SYRIAN BREAD SALAD *Fa-toosh*

- 2 loaves Syrian bread *marquq*
- 1/2 bunch green onions
- 1/2 bunch parsley
- 1 cucumber
- 1/2 bunch fresh mint
   (or 2 tablespoons dried)
- 2 tablespoons fresh cilentro (optional)
- 1 teaspoon salt
- 1/2 teaspoon pepper
- Juice of 3 lemons
- 1/2 cup olive oil
- Black olives

Break unsoftened Syrian Bread into bite-size pieces. Cut all vegetables into small pieces. Mix vegetables with bread in salad bowl. Add salt, pepper, lemon juice, and oil and mix well. Garnish with black olives. *Serves 6*.

SYRIAN POTATO SALAD *Batata arabee salata*

1 pound potatoes
Olive oil
Juice of 3 lemons
1 onion, chopped
Salt and pepper to taste

2 tablespoons chopped parsley
Olives
2 tomatoes, sliced
1 tablespoon dried mint

Boil potatoes, then peel and cube. Coat with olive oil. Add lemon juice, onion, salt and pepper. Garnish with parsley, olives, tomatoes, and mint. *Serves 4.*

TOMATO SARDINE SALAD *Salata banadoora-samek*

4 tomatoes
1 small can sardines
Lettuce

1 medium onion, sliced thinly
2 tablespoons lemon juice
1 tablespoon chopped parsley or chives

Peel tomatoes, slice, and chill. Drain oil from sardines, remove skin and back-bone. Arrange lettuce on salad plate; place tomatoes on lettuce, cover with sardines and onion slices and sprinkle with lemon juice. Garnish with parsley or chives. *Serves 4.*

RICE-PASTA SALAD (China joins the Middle East with this popular take-along salad)

8 oz. vermicelli twisted pasta
1 cup rice
1/2 cup butter
1 can french onion soup

1 can chicken broth
1/2 cup water
1 teaspoon soy sauce
1 can water chestnut

Break up pasta and saute with rice in butter until pasta is brown. Mix together rest of ingredients and place in a two quart casserole. Bake in preheated 325º oven for 45 minutes.

BROCCOLI-PASTA SALAD *(A great luncheon served with Grilled Chicken)*

2 cups penne pasta
1 cup broccoli florets
1 bermuda onion, thinly sliced
1 tomato, wedged
1 small avocado, wedged

6 sprigs parsley, chopped
3 tablespoons olive oil
1 tablespoon wine vinegar
Juice of 1 lemon
Salt and pepper to taste
1/8 pound feta cheese

Cook pasta in boiling salted water until done. Cool and place in a salad bowl. Mix in all the ingredients exept feta cheese. Arrange on individual salad plates lined with romaine lettuce and top with feta cheese. *Serves 6.*

NOODLE-CABBAGE-ALMOND SALAD *Raves for this crunchy salad*

- 1 2.8 oz. package ramen pride chicken flavored noodles
- 1 head of cabbage (about 1-1/4 pound)
- 4 green onions, chopped
- 3 teaspoon sesame seeds
- 1/2 cup slivered almonds

Preheat oven to 500°. Break apart noodles, place in baking tray and toast five minutes. Stir and continue to toast five more minutes until all noodles are golden brown. Remove from oven and toast lightly the sesame seeds and almonds until golden. Set to one side.

Dressing: **Mix together: 2 tablespoons sugar - 1/2 teaspoon pepper - 3 tablespoons rice vinegar - 1 teaspoon salt and 1/2 cup salad oil.**

Heat dressing to dissolve sugar. Remove from fire. When cool, mix in the packet flavoring that came with the noodles. Pour dressing over cabbage before serving. Add sesame and noodles and toss. *Yield: 6 servings. Serve in a platter lined with raddichio lettuce and sprinkle a few more toasted almonds on top for a pretty picture.*

CHIC PEA SALAD *Homos salata*

- 2 cups canned chic peas, drained
- 1 tomato, diced
- 1 green pepper, seeded and chopped
- 1 yellow pepper, seeded and chopped
- 2 cloves garlic, mashed in salt
- 2 teaspoons olive oil
- 2 tablespoons lemon juice
- Salt and pepper to taste

In a large salad bowl, mix together all of the above ingredients. *Serve on a bed of lettuce leaves. Serves 4-6.*

PASTA with WATERCRESS *Ma'karun ma' jirjeeree*

- 1 bunch watercress
- 1 pound pasta shells
- 1 sweet red pepper, seeded
- 2 cloves garlic
- 1/4 cup pine nuts
- 1 teaspoon lemon juice
- 1 teaspoon wine vinegar
- 3 tablespoons olive oil
- Salt and pepper to taste

Rinse the watercress. Shake out excess water. Cook pasta in hot salted water until done. Chop red pepper. Mash garlic in salt. Saute pine nuts in a sprayed non-stick skillet until golden. Place all ingredients in salad bowl. Add the cooked pasta shells to the watercress mixture and enjoy.

OLIVE OIL

Zite Il Zitoon

There is a great deal of biblical significance in the highly revered olive trees. My Uncle, the late Right Reverend George Ghannam, as a monk at the St. George Monastery in Syria, planted a grove of olive trees. He told our family stories that have been written in the tabloids of many biblical historians. Of the ancient olive trees that sheltered Jesus and His Disciples many times in the Garden of Gethsemane. The name of the Mount of Olives comes from trees that are scattered from that location to the shores of Palestine, from Beirut to Sidon and the neighborhood of Jaffa and is covered with olive-groves. There are some 50 to 60 varieties of the green olive tree that originated in Syria and Asia Minor's coastal regions. History records olive trees also in Egypt, Greece, Turkey, Lebanon, Palestine, Spain, Italy and France.

Known as **the** cooking oil of the Middle East, there are dozens of varieties to choose from. The **extra virgin olive oil** comes from olives that are harvested by hand. This glorious fruit is a staple to both rich and poor in the Middle East.. Long thin poles are used by men and women to beat the olives from the tree, while children climb trees, shaking the boughs. To keep the trees from being damaged by the beating and shaking, a full crop is picked only every other year. The olives are washed and pressed to extract the oil, known as the first pressing or cold-pressing. The color ranges from a rich green gold to a pale-green color. This is used more for drizzling over cooked food and to flavor salad dressings, i.e., *tabooley, ful imdamis, fatoush, salata*.

Virgin oil is used in the same way as extra virgin oil.

Olive oil. This is an economical choice to use for cooking many of these foods.

Light oil is lighter in flavor and color but **not** lower in calories or fat than other olive oils. This refined olive oil is highly filtered and contains a small amount of the virgin oil. In recipes, you can use this as any other vegetable oil.

A popular breakfast in the Middle East is dipping Arabic bread in a bowl and scooping up *za'tar* mixed with olive oil or baked *Mana'eesh* bread (dough topped with *za'tar* and olive oil). Another favorite is a bowl of yogurt cheese balls *labanee* preserved in olive oil and used as a spread on pocket bread or thin Arabic bread *marqooq.* (eaten also as a snack or light lunch with a salad)

One thing to keep in mind - olive oil will become rancid if not used within a month or two. It is wise to buy small containers unless used daily.

Delicately flavored at this first pressing of ripe olives, olive oil is used not only for cooking, but for making soap. Some of the larger olive trees yield as much as 12 gallons of oil. Olive oil of various qualities is exported all over the world.

Sold as souvenirs in Jerusalem, Palestine and Damascus are many articles carved from olive-wood.

CARE OF BLACK OLIVES *Zitoon aswad*

Middle Eastern food stores feature olives in huge earthen barrels topped with wooden covers. The olives are preserved in salt and water They can be purchased by the pound from stores listed in the Shoppers' Guide. Olives will keep for many days. Rinse with cold water and fill a half gallon jar with the olives. Pour cold water over the olives. Add 1/4 cup olive oil and 3 tablespoons vinegar.

FRESH GREEN OLIVES *Zitoon akhthar*

Slash each olive on one side. Place in crock. Sprinkle salt over olives. Mix every day for 8 days. After 8 days, salt will draw. Empty liquid from crock. Cover crock with platter. Olives are ripe when color turns dark. When ripe, add olive oil and lemon slices. For an added flavor, mix in some dried thyme.

Platter of baklawa

Platter of stuffed vegetables

Another party favorite alongside Mansef is this platter of Lahum Mishwee, Mowaseer, and Djaj on a bed of rice-orzo.

MANSEF PARTIES

If you are as adventuresome as I am, you can have your own *MANSEF* party. After an invitation to San Diego by relatives of King Abu Faisal of **Saudi Arabia** and another sponsored by the University of Arizona's Arab League students, I became addicted to *Mansef*. My guest list is endless when friends want to be included in this festive party. *Mansef* actually means a large communal tray on which is mounded chunks of cooked lamb and rice over Arabic bread (called *Shrak* by the Jordanians and *marquq* by the Syrians) and enhanced by a yogurt sauce and pine nuts. From **Saudia Arabia, Morocco and Jordan**, this ancient ritual in a Bedouin tent is a compliment to anyone invited to a *Mansef* dinner. There is an art to using the right hand and deftly rolling a ball of rice around a piece of lamb, then popping the mixture into the mouth.

I've modernized this ritual somewhat. My guests sit on the floor around plush cushions, a Middle Eastern tablecloth accentuates the setting along with caftans worn by the ladies, and I manage to have on hand some Bedouin's romantic headdresses *Kuffiyahs* for the men. Dinner plates and utensils are available for those that can't master the art of eating with their fingers. Following the meal, several bowls of warm water are passed around so guests can wash their hands. Wet napkins are also appropriate.

Guests look forward eagerly to drinking their freshly ground Arabic coffee. Once consumed, the hostess is ready to read their fortunes from the pattern formed in the inverted cup by the sediment that remains in the cup. All the while, the lilting strings of the lute can be heard in the background, getting ready for the evening's entertainment with some Arabic dancing.

(If you are attempting your own party, roast a baby lamb, about 3 months old and adjust your recipe for the amount of your guests). Although the **Palestinians and Jordanians** use *jameed* a sun-dried, reconstituted yogurt and much thinner in consistency, the Arab American kitchen uses a tasty substitute of fresh yogurt cooked with a little cornstarch.

MANSEF, A Bedouin feast

2 pounds lamb, cut in cubes 2-1/2"
2 teaspoons salt
1-1/2 teaspoon black pepper
1-1/2 teaspoon allspice
1 tablespoon ground
   cardamon (optional)
2 onions, sliced
4 cups yogurt

2 tablespoons cornstarch
Pinch of saffron
6 tablespoons butter
4 cups rice
1/2 cup pine nuts
6 sprigs parsley
8 loaves of Arabic bread *marquq or shrak*

Cover lamb with water in kettle and place over medium fire. Add onion, salt, pepper, allspice and cardamon. Cover and cook for 30 minutes.

In separate pan place yogurt. Mix cornstarch with a little water to make paste. Add to the yogurt and mix well. Cook on medium heat, stirring constantly until it boils. Mix the boiled lamb with the yogurt and add saffron or turmeric to give the mixture a light yellow color. Simmer for 40 minutes until meat is tender and yogurt is thick. Reserve extra broth for finale.

Boil 8 cups of water. Add 2 teaspoons salt and the 6 tablespoons butter. Add 4 cups rice. Cover and boil for 5 minutes, then simmer until rice is cooked, about 20 minutes. Saute pine nuts in 2 teaspoons oil until golden shade. Place to one side. Mix together with the chopped parsley.

Take loaves of Arabic bread and place over large serving trays. Spoon some of the yogurt-meat broth over the bread. Pile the rice on top into a mound leaving 1-inch of bread showing. Cover the rice with the lamb and top that with more of the yogurt sauce. Sprinkle pine nut-parsley mixture over all. Have several sauce boats on hand to pass yogurt sauce around for those who wish to spoon over their individual servings. *Serves 10*.

MEATS OF THE MIDDLE EAST

AND THE WONDERFUL DAYS AT THE
Mahrajan

Women of the Middle East know a thousand and one ways to make meats tasty. Marinated and seasoned with spices and herbs, meats are slowly cooked to bring out the flavor.

During the feasting season, the head of the family goes to the country to bargain with a farmer for a spring lamb. At home the lamb is fattened for a week on mulberry leaves and malt. Then the family, neighbors, and relatives all gather to slaughter the lamb. The lamb is dressed and rubbed with a handful of spices and herbs, tied on a spit and rotated over coals. As it starts to brown, the lamb is basted with hot fat. Sometimes lambs are stuffed with Minced Lamb-Rice dressing and served whole on platters surrounded by fruit.

As children, sister Kate, brother Bob and I eagerly looked forward to Dad taking us once a month to the Shaheen farm in anticipation of a hay ride while the men were shearing the lamb. We no sooner went home with a side of lamb, Dad would section it for the many intriguing dishes Mom prepared. Visiting Bishops called her preparation of lamb liver, a food fit for the Kings. And although it took a great deal of time to stuff *Ghumee and Thilla'* with a lamb-rice mixture, the end result was well worth it.

One has only to ask a butcher in your neighborhood for a leg of lamb or lamb shoulder for making some of the tempting lamb additions to stews, with potatoes, and with cracked wheat. Offering the most tender meat is the leg of lamb used for making *kibby and lahum mishwee (Shish Kebab)*. Lamb bones are cracked and used in preparing some of the recipes. Placed on the bottom of the pan when cooking Stuffed Cabbage Leaves, they enhance the flavor. Meat from the shoulder or breast of lamb, a less expensive cut, is used to stuff grape and cabbage leaves, squash and eggplant.

Throughout America, Syrians and Lebanese, Orthodox, Maronites, Melkites, Roman Catholics and other religious denominations journeyed every year to Carey, Ohio to the *mahrajan* (outdoor festival). This was in conjunction with a pilgrimage to the feast day of the Falling Asleep of the Theotokos (Feast of the Assumption of the Blessed Mother) on August 15th. Joining a caravan of cars, relatives and friends planned this particular weekend as a family vacation, renewing acquaintances from throughout the country. Thousands of families came to pray at this pilgrimage. The chapel was set aside in a special building where prayers were said for the miraculous healing of the sick as worshippers crawled for miles on their knees as they approached the tomb of the Blessed Virgin Mother.

On nearby grounds, picnic tables were made available to all the visitors. There was an atmosphere of the *mahrajan* as arabic music played to the strings of the lute and rhythms poured forth by *derbukkis* (drums). The young clasped hands and in a semi-circle danced the *dubkee* while the elderly men found tables to play their favorite card game of *whist*. Meanwhile, Mom and all the other ladies were preparing picnic tables laden with baskets of food they brought from home - *tabooley, fatayer laban, sabanigh, homos, za'tar, sfeeha,* along with everyone's favorite anise filled bread *Ka'ick,* fresh fruit and pastries. The aroma of *lahum mishwee* permeated the air as men of that region bar-b-qued the lamb for arriving guests.

As the evening approached, stories were exchanged of these immigrants who came to the land of the free that was now their home, the land they loved and learned to call their America.

And all the while, the aroma of the barbecued lamb lingered in the air as the food stands prepared to close - for a few hour's rest before another day at the *mahrajan*.

For spiritual blessings in another area of the country, Orthodox parishioners eagerly look forward to joining caravans of cars and buses traveling great distances to the St. Thekla Pilgrimage that takes place every September at the Antiochian Village in Bolivar, Pennsylvania. Stopping on the way, friends gather at picnic grounds to share their *zawadee of fatayer* and picnic baskets with one another before continuing their journey to strengthen their Christian fellowship, spirituality, and inspiration at this magnificent setting in the mountains where everyone rejoices in God's love. How joyous and awesome it is to drive into the village grounds seeing the sky merging with the hillside overlooking the valley - the wooded setting - the stone altar; a perfect setting fashioned by the hand of God. Exhilarating and peaceful to stand for a moment and listen to choirs rehearsing. And then on Sunday in an open air service witnessing His Eminence and the Clergy partaking of the Holy Eucharist and embracing one another "for the love of God." As I watched this beautiful personal relationship with our Creator, it took my imaginative mind back to a time and place in history watching the Lord and His Disciples at the Last Supper. Those are moments one never forgets.

MEATS OF THE MIDDLE EAST (although lamb is preferred, beef may be substituted in these recipes).

ROAST LEG OF LAMB *Fakheth lahum ghanum* (Is. 53:7 Ps. 95:7)

5 pound leg of lamb
1 teaspoon salt
2 cloves garlic, minced

1/4 teaspoon each pepper, marjoram, sage, ginger, thyme
1 tablespoon olive oil

Wipe lamb with damp cloth. Cut small gashes 1/4-inch long on top surface of lamb. Combine remaining ingredients except olive oil. Rub well into meat so that all gashes are completely filled. Give roast a final coating with oil. Sear in preheated oven (500°) F. for 15 minutes. Reduce temperature to 350° F. and roast about 1-1/2 hours. (If desired, add par-boiled potatoes and onions to roasting pan when meat is half-cooked) *Serves 6-8*

LAMB BURGERS *Mow-a-seer*—also known as *Kafta (photo on page 38)*

1 pound lamb, ground twice
1/2 bunch parsley, chopped

1 onion, chopped fine
Thyme, salt, pepper
1 teaspoon lemon juice

Combine all ingredients. Form on a skewer or make rolls about 6 inches long. Place in dry baking pan and bake in moderate oven (350°) F. approximately 20 minutes. *Serves 4.*

LAMB BURGERS WITH PINE NUTS *Kafta snoober*

1 pound ground lamb
4 tablespoons chopped parsley
1 onion, minced
1 teaspoon dried mint

Salt and pepper to taste
2 teaspoons butter
1/4 cup pine nuts, sauteed in butter to a golden shade
1 12-ounce can tomato puree

Mix together lamb, parsley, onion, mint, salt and pepper. Shape into rolls, filling each with 1 teaspoon pine nuts. Place in baking pan and pour tomato puree over rolls. Bake for 30 minutes in moderate oven (350°) F. *Serves 4.*

BOILED BEEF TONGUE *Sane il buqqar*

3-4 pound fresh beef tongue
1 clove garlic
1 bay leaf

1 tablespoon cloves, whole
1 teaspoon allspice, whole

Cover tongue with cold water and cook until water boils. Discard water and cover with fresh water. Add remaining ingredients and cook in covered pan on low heat for 3 hours. Skin and slice tongue. Serve with *Taratoor*. *Serves 5.* (This is excellent for company .. use in salad or sliced as sandwiches tucked in pocket bread or with a *tahini* sauce.)

LAMB DUMPLINGS WITH YOGURT SAUCE *Sheesh barak*

3 cups flour
1 pound lamb, coarsely ground
1 onion, chopped fine

Salt, pepper, allspice
Coriander (optional)

Knead flour well with a pinch of salt and about 3/4 cup water. Roll dough and cut into 2-inch rounds. Combine meat, onion, salt, pepper, allspice, and coriander. Place on rounds of dough. Fold each in half and close edges. Twist around your finger into the shape of a hat.

SAUCE FOR *SHEESH BARAK*

    3 quarts yogurt   1/2 teaspoon salt
    1 tablespoon flour and 1 egg white   1 tablespoon dried mint
    2 cloves garlic   1/4 cup butter

Combine yogurt, flour and egg white. Beat mixture thoroughly. Place pan on medium fire and stir constantly until yogurt comes to a boil. Immerse dumplings and let cook in yogurt about 20 minutes on a low fire. Mash garlic with 1/2 teaspoon salt and 1 tablespoon dried mint. Saute garlic mixture in melted butter for a few seconds, then pour over the dumplings. *Serves 6.*

LAMB LIVER   *Qasabee imhamatha*

    1 pound lamb liver   1/2 cup water
    1 onion, chopped   2 cloves garlic, crushed
    3 tablespoons butter   Salt and pepper to taste
    1 cup tomato puree

Rinse liver thoroughly in cold water. Boil approximately 15 minutes. Rinse again. Chop into small pieces. Brown onion in butter. Add liver and simmer. Add tomato puree and 1/2 cup water. Add crushed garlic, salt, and pepper. Cook approximately 15 minutes longer. *Serves 4-5.*

LAMB BAKED WITH POTATOES   *Lahum bil saneeyee*

    1 pound lamb, cubed   2 onions, sliced
    1/4 pound butter   1 12-ounce can tomato puree
    3 large potatoes, sliced   Salt and pepper to taste

Alternate layers of lamb, potatoes, and onions in well-buttered baking pan and dot with butter. Pour tomato puree on top and add seasonings. Bake in slow oven (250°) F. for approximately 30 minutes. *Serves 5-6.* This is an excellent LENTEN dish. Just omit the lamb.

LAMB AND MUSHROOMS   *Ghanum ma' fotir*

    1 pound lamb, cubed   1/2 cup hot water
    4 onions, minced   Salt and pepper to taste
    2 tablespoons butter   Pinch of rosemary
    1 pound fresh mushrooms, cut in half (or 1-pound can of mushrooms)

Brown lamb and onions in butter. Saute mushrooms in butter. Add to lamb and onions. Add hot water, cover and simmer 10 to 15 minutes. Add salt, pepper, and rosemary. Cook over low fire for about 10 minutes. If liquid texture is desired, add more water. *Serves 5.*

LAMB STEW *Yukhnee*

> 2 pounds lamb, cubed
> 1/2 cup butter
> 2 onions, chopped
> 1 clove garlic
> Salt and pepper to taste
> 1/2 cup tomato puree
> 3 large potatoes, cubed

Saute meat until brown in melted butter. Remove meat from skillet and brown onions and garlic in remaining butter. Add seasonings and tomato puree and cook together for a few minutes. Return meat to skillet. Add enough water to cover and cook over medium heat for about 1 hour or until meat is almost done. Add potatoes. Boil until potatoes are cooked, about 30 minutes. *Serves 6-8.*

LAMB TRIPE *Ghumee*

> 1 tripe
> 3 teaspoons baking soda in 2 cups water
> 1 cup chopped lamb
> 1/2 cup shelled chick-peas
> 1 cup rice
> 4 tablespoons melted butter
> Salt and pepper to taste
> Dash each of cloves and cinnamon
> 2 bay leaves

Soak tripe in baking soda water for several hours. Drain and clean thoroughly. Rinse rice in water. Combine lamb, chick-peas, rice, butter, salt, pepper and cinnamon. Make pocket out of 2 or 3 pieces of the tripe. Stuff with lamb-rice mixture and sew together. Place in boiling water and add bay leaves. Cook about 40 minutes. Remove bay leaves. Serve liquid as soup garnished with dried mint. *Serves 6-8.*

LAMB ON SKEWERS *Shish kebab or lahum mishwee*

> 3 pounds boned lean leg of lamb
>   or sirloin steak
> 3 large onions, quartered
> 1 cup red wine
> 3 tablespoons oil
> 1 tablespoon dried mint
> Salt and pepper to taste
> 4 green peppers, wedged
> 5-6 medium firm tomatoes, wedged

Cut lamb or steak into 1-1/2" cubes. Make a marinade of wine, oil and mint in a deep dish and marinate meat and vegetables for at least 2 hours, preferably overnight. Season when ready to broil. Arrange lamb cubes on skewers, alternating with onion, pepper slices and tomatoes. Broil slowly over hot charcoal or in broiler of kitchen range, about 10 minutes on the rare side and 15 minutes for medium rare. Turn skewers frequently. *Serves 8-10* **Armenians** *call this Shashlik.*

MEAT-EGG ROLL *Znood il banat*

2 pounds lamb or beef, ground twice
1 onion, chopped
Salt and pepper to taste
5 hard-cooked eggs
Butter

Mix together lamb, onion and seasoning. Pat out meat mixture in a rectangle. Place eggs on meat mixture. Roll meat around egg. Close at edges. Place in buttered pan. Brush top with melted butter and bake in moderate oven (350°) F. until brown, about 20 minutes. *Serves 5.*

LAMB WITH YOGURT *Shik-ree-yee or Laban immoo*

1/2 pound lamb chunks
1 onion, chopped
Butter
1 quart yogurt
1 tablespoon flour
1 clove garlic, crushed
1 tablespoon dried mint
Salt to taste

Boil lamb chunks in water in covered pan about 30 minutes. Drain, and reserve broth. Brown onion in butter and add lamb chunks. Stir yogurt in a separate pan until smooth.

Add a little water to the flour to make a paste and add to yogurt. Cook over low fire, stirring constantly to keep from burning. When it begins to thicken, add lamb and onions. Add garlic, mint and salt. If yogurt gets too thick, thin with lamb broth. *Serves 4.*

VEAL BREAST *Thilla'*

1 tablespoon salt
2 teaspoons baking soda
1-1/2 cup water
5 pound breast of veal
2 cups rice
4 tablespoons Clarified Butter
1 cup chick-peas, canned (or prepared fresh chick-peas)
Salt and pepper to taste
Pinch each of cloves and allspice

Soak veal in water with salt and baking soda about 1-1/2 hours. Drain and pat dry with paper towels. Cut pocket in breast. Soak rice in lukewarm water 15 minutes. Drain. Then simmer rice in butter 2 minutes, stirring constantly. Add 3-1/2 cups boiling water to rice. Cover pan and cook 15 minutes on medium fire. Mix rice with chick-peas, salt, pepper, and spices. Stuff loosely into veal breast. Sew opening. Place in roaster and bake in moderate oven (350°) F. allowing 35 minutes per pound. *Serves 6-8.*

BREAST OF LAMB, STUFFED *Ghanum mihshee (Is. 53:7)*

Lamb breasts can be substituted for veal, using 4 breasts of lamb and slitting the breast between ribs and meat to form a cavity. The cavity should be stuffed loosely allowing the rice to expand. In this particular recipe use uncooked rice mixed with chick-peas. Follow above procedure of sewing up the cavity. Place the breasts in a deep pan, covering them with water. Add salt and bring to a boil. Remove scum on top and then cook approximately 45 minutes on low heat. Remove from broth and place in baking tray. Place in preheated oven (400°) and bake 20 minutes until breasts are brown.

KIDNEYS *Kilwat ghanum mishwee*

1/2 pound Lamb kidneys	1/2 teaspoon salt
Butter	1/2 teaspoon garlic powder

Cut kidneys in half but do not separate completely. Remove skin. Brush with melted butter, salt, and garlic powder. Grill over a very hot fire 5 to 7 minutes. They should be underdone. Serve with watercress. *Serves 2.*

BABY LAMB, STUFFED *Kharoof mihshee (Matt. 25:32,33)*

15-20 pound baby spring lamb	5 cups boiling water
6 pounds coarsely ground lamb	3 cups long grain rice
4 tablespoons butter	1 teaspoon each of allspice and cinnamon
1 cup pine nuts	1 tablespoon salt

Order the lamb from your meat market, ready for roasting. It should be cleaned and trimmed and ready to be stuffed. Rub the lamb inside and out with salt.

In a large saucepan, melt the butter and saute the ground lamb, stirring until browned. Add pine nuts and saute until golden. Add rice and seasonings plus 5 cups of boiling water, stirring ingredients together. When it comes to a boil, reduce heat, cover the pan and cook about 20 minutes until liquid is absorbed. Set to one side to cool.

Fill cavity of lamb with the stuffing and sew opening together with heavy white thread. Tie together both front and back legs.

Bake in a preheated 350° oven in an uncovered roasting pan. Baste in its own juices until tender, about 30 minutes per pound. *Serves 15 to 20.*

QAWARMA

1 leg of lamb or lamb shoulder

Ask your butcher to debone the lamb and chop it in half. Save the bone for cooking stuffed vegetables. Strip off the fat, mince it and boil down until it is of smooth texture like lard. Strain any particles that might remain. Discard the particles.

Chop the meat finely, then boil the meat in the fat. When it turns brown, place the fat and meat in crocks and store in the refrigerator. Use it to fry scrambled eggs. Try sprinkling some cumin powder on top of the eggs. Tear off a piece of Syrian bread and scoop up the *bythot ma' qawarma* (eggs and meat) for a mouth-watering tasty breakfast.

Lamb Burgers *mow-a-seer*
on the grill
—recipe on page 33.

BRAINS PREPARED FOR COOKING *Inkha matbookh*

Prepare brains for cooking by covering with cold water and soaking for 1 hour. Remove membranes and parboil for 20 minutes in salted water to which 1 tablespoon vinegar has been added. Drain. When cool, place in cold water and separate into small pieces.

SCRAMBLED BRAINS AND EGGS *Inkha ma' bythot*

Fry 1 cup Brains Prepared For Cooking in butter or margarine until brown. Add 3 whole eggs, sprinkle lightly with salt, and scramble mixture by stirring with fork. Garnish with *kamoun* (powdered cuminseed). *Serves 4.*

FRIED BRAINS *Inkha miqlee*

1 pound Brains Prepared For Cooking
1 egg
1/4 pound butter

Dip brains in bread crumbs, then in slightly beaten egg, and in crumbs again. Fry until golden brown on all sides. *Serves 4.*

BAKED BRAINS WITH SAUCE *Inkha mishwee ma' marqeh*

1 -1 1/2 pounds Brains Prepared For Cooking
2 tablespoons butter
2 tablespoons chopped onion
2 tablespoons flour
Salt and pepper to taste
1/2 cup water or stock
1 cup cooked tomatoes
2 tablespoons each celery and green pepper, chopped
1 bay leaf
1 sprig thyme

Brown onion in butter. Sift together flour, salt and pepper and add to onion. Cook, stirring constantly, until thickened. Add water or stock and tomatoes. Stir until blended. Lower heat and add celery, green pepper, bay leaf, and thyme. Cook for 10 minutes, stirring occasionally. If necessary, add more water. Remove bay leaf and thyme and add brains. Bake in moderate oven (350°) for 15 minutes. *Serves 4-6.*

Rice-ring mold topped with pine nuts garnished with tomatoes, mint, and olives

Red Snapper (Sultan Abrahim) Platter of tahini and Baba ghanouj sauces Garnishes: pomegranate seeds, lemon, parsley —recipe on page 110

GAME, POULTRY, AND DRESSINGS

Djaj il Arth wa Hashwa

One of the most succulent chicken dishes comes from **Jordan**. It is their legendary *Musakhan,* simmered and then baked to crispiness, the chickens are topped with fresh sumac powder, olive oil and lots of red onions and sauteed pine nuts.

In Syria and Lebanon, every housewife has learned the preparation of chickens that are moist, rubbing them inside and out with spices, then stuffing either with *hashwa ghanum ma' snoober* (a mixture of minced lamb and pine nuts or with a mixture of rice, giblets and walnuts). Timing isn't checked by the clock; tenderness is determined by poking and pinching. The chicken is then roasted golden brown in the oven.

Ducks and pigeons are plentiful in Egypt and a roast duck stuffed with cracked wheat and basted with orange juice is an Egyptian dish served for special occasions. **(Luke 2:24)**

Considered a delicacy in Syria and Lebanon are pigeons roasted whole or cooked in a stew with rice, almonds, and raisins.

The accent on foods with spices and seasonings is embedded in geography and one dish that becomes versatile is the *couscous;* across the breadth of North Africa, *couscous* is a staple food, and a main dish in Egypt.

ROAST PHEASANT *Djaj il arth*

2-1/2 pound pheasant　　　　　　　1/2 teaspoon cinnamon
1/2 teaspoon salt　　　　　　　　　Salad oil
1/2 teaspoon pepper

Clean and dry the pheasant thoroughly. Rub cavity with salt, pepper, and cinnamon. Bake uncovered in a moderately hot oven (400°) for 20 minutes. Place several thicknesses of cheesecloth, soaked in salad oil, on the breast of the pheasant. Cover and bake in slow oven (250°) for 2 hours. Serve with Rice-walnut Dressing. *Serves 3.*

ROAST CHICKEN *Djaj mishwee*

5-pound chicken
1 tablespoon salt
1/4 teaspoon each of cinnamon, nutmeg, allspice, salt and pepper

Clean the chicken. Tie legs together. Place in pan and cover with water. Add 1 tablespoon salt. Cover and cook until tender, about 40 minutes. Preheat oven to 350°. Remove chicken and rub cavity with spices. Roast in moderate oven (350°) for 30 minutes, using chicken broth to baste. Chicken will turn a golden brown. *Serves 4.* Reserve broth for rice dishes. **(Matt. 23:37)**

ROAST CHICKEN WITH RICE-GIBLET STUFFING *Djaj mihshee ma' hashwa roz*

5 pound chicken
1/2 pound giblets, chopped
3 tablespoons butter
1 cup rice
1/2 cup chopped English walnuts, blanched
1/2 teaspoon salt
1/8 teaspoon each of allspice, nutmeg, cinnamon, pepper

Clean the chicken. Saute giblets in butter. Add rice and stir constantly for 3 minutes. Remove from heat and add blanched walnuts, salt and spices. Stuff chicken loosely. Truss, tie legs together and place in a kettle. Cover with water and simmer until almost tender, 40 minutes. Preheat oven to 300°. Remove chicken from kettle and roast in an open pan in slow oven 325° for 1/2 hour or until chicken is tender. Last 10 minutes of roasting, glaze chicken with butter to turn a golden brown. *Serves 6.*

DUCK WITH WINE SAUCE *But ma' marqeh*

1 duck
2 tablespoons butter
1 onion, chopped
1 cup red wine
1 cup tomato sauce
1 cup water
Dash of cinnamon
Salt and pepper to taste

Wash and clean duck and cut into serving pieces. Saute onion in butter, add duck, and brown on all sides. Add wine, cover, and cook for 20 minutes. Add tomato sauce diluted with 1 cup water, cinnamon, salt and pepper. Cover and simmer until duck is cooked, approximately 30 minutes. Sauce may be thickened with a little flour if desired. *Serves 4.*

ROAST GOOSE *Wuz*

7-8 pound goose
1 apple, quartered
2 onions, quartered

Singe, wash, and clean goose. Stuff cavity with the apple and onions. Prick with fork through the fat layers of the goose. This will help to draw out the fat. Place in shallow pan in moderately hot oven (375°) for 15 to 20 minutes or until fat starts to run. Remove from oven, pour off fat. Repeat this 2 or 3 times until fat ceases to drip. The bird is well cooked when thick portion of drumstick meat is soft. (For a 7-8 pound goose, roast 30 minutes per pound). Do not add water and do not baste. Discard apples and onions after roasting. *Serves 6.*

TURKEY *Habesh*   (This recipe is sure to give you a moist turkey every time.)

25 pound turkey
2 tablespoons baking soda
1/4 teaspoon each of cinnamon, nutmeg, allspice, salt and pepper

Soak turkey overnight in pan of water to which baking soda has been added. Following day rinse thoroughly. Place in large kettle and parboil until tender. Remove from turkey broth and dry. Reserve broth. Preheat oven to 250°. Rub inside and out with spices. Place turkey in roasting pan with small amount of broth. Cover with aluminum foil. Bake in slow oven (250°) 2 to 2-1/2 hours, basting occasionally with broth. When turkey turns golden brown, remove from oven. Triple the recipe for Rice-Giblet Dressing and serve with the turkey. Serves 12.

FRIED RABBIT   *Aranabee miqlee*

2 rabbits	**1/4 teaspoon pepper**
4 tablespoons flour	**6 tablespoons salad oil**
2 teaspoons salt	**4 tablespoons hot water**

Clean rabbits and cut up for frying. Combine flour, salt, and pepper. Dredge rabbit pieces until well coated. Brown on all sides in oil in a covered skillet. When well browned, sprinkle with hot water. Cover and simmer over low heat for 45 minutes or until tender. *Serves 4.*

MARINATED BROILED CHICKEN   *Djaj ma' limoon wa za'tar*

2 - 4 pound fryers, sectioned	**2 tablespoons thyme**
1/2 - 3/4 cup salad oil	**1 teaspoon powdered garlic**
2/3 cup lemon juice	**Salt and pepper to taste**

Clean chicken thoroughly. Place in large bowl. Mix together rest of ingredients to make a marinade. Pour on chicken and mix with hands. Marinate for 1 hour or overnight if using chicken next day. Arrange chicken in baking tray. Preheat oven to 350°. Bake for 1 hour, then broil until golden brown, about 15 minutes. *Serves 6.*

CHICKEN STEW *Yukhnet djaj*

1 tablespoon baking soda	2 large potatoes, cubed
1 cup fresh chick-peas *homos*	1 teaspoon salt
(or 1 cup canned chick peas)	1/2 teaspoon pepper
3-4 pound fryer, sectioned	
4 onions, quartered	

Soak fresh chick-peas with baking soda in water overnight. Drain chick-peas, cover with water, and add chicken pieces. Cover pan and simmer on low fire 45 minutes until tender, skimming top of scum. Then add onions, potatoes, and seasonings and cook 25 minutes more. (If using canned chick peas, add to chicken the same time with onions and potatoes). Delicious served over Rice-Orzo Dressing. *Serves 6.* You won't have any left-overs on this one - the children relish it as well as the adults.

BAKED CHICKEN WITH SUMAC *Musakhan*

In **Jordan,** people line up blocks long waiting for this popular dish.

2 broilers, 3-1/2 pounds each	1/2 cup pine nuts
4 cups red onions, julienned	8 tablespoons *sumac**
1/2 cup olive oil	Salt and pepper to taste

Parboil chickens about 30 minutes. Remove from broth and sprinkle salt and pepper over them. Place in baking tray and sprinkle sumac generously over the top of the chickens. Bake in 350° preheated oven for 40 minutes. While chickens are baking, simmer onions in hot olive oil for 3 minutes. Remove onions and add pine nuts to skillet, stirring and watching carefully so they do not burn. Remove from skillet as soon as they appear a light golden shade.

Place Syrian thin bread *marquq, Jordanian shrak* on large platter. Ladle onions and oil generously on bread. Place chickens on top of onions. Then add more onions and oil on top of chicken. Sprinkle pine nuts over all. *Serves 6.*

*Sumac is pungent in taste - grows in the desserts of the Middle East. (If you like lemon, you'll like this even better).

CHICKEN WITH OKRA *Djaj wa Baymee*

1 2-1/2 pound chicken	4 sprigs parsley
1 pound okra	1/2 teaspoon each of thyme and basil
Butter	1 teaspoon salt
1 large onion	1/2 teaspoon pepper
2 cloves garlic	4 tablespoons lemon juice
1 cup tomatoes, whole	

Boil chicken until cooked. While chicken is cooking, saute okra in butter. Remove chicken from pan and cool. When cool, shred chicken. Add to rest of ingredients except okra and cook for 20 minutes. Then add okra and lemon juice and cook in covered kettle another 10 minutes. *Serves 6 to 8.*

MINCED LAMB-RICE DRESSING *Hashwa ghanum ma' snoober*

    1/2 pound lamb, minced   **1/4 cup rice, cooked 15 minutes in 1/4**
    1/4 cup pine nuts   **cup water**
    1/4 pound butter   **Salt and pepper to taste**

Saute lamb and pine nuts in butter. Place in a bowl and add rice, salt and pepper. Use to stuff a 5-pound chicken. Or omit the rice and use as a tasty dressing over a platter of *Kibby neeyee*.

GIBLET-BREAD STUFFING with CHESTNUTS *Hashwa qiwanis ma' khobaz wa kastana*

    2 cups giblets, cooked   **1/4 teaspoon pepper**
    1 cup turkey broth   **1 tablespoon poultry seasoning**
    1 pound chestnuts (optional)   **1-1/2 teaspoons each of prepared mustard,**
    3/4 cup butter or margarine   **diced celery, minced parsley, sage**
    1/2 cup minced onion   **3 quarts day-old bread crumbs, toasted**

Chop giblets. Combine the turkey broth, butter, and onion and simmer 5 minutes. Roast the chestnuts. Peel and add along with the other ingredients to the giblets. Place in baking tray and bake about 30 minutes in moderately hot oven (350°); or use this to stuff cavity of an 8 pound bird. *Serves 6.*

CLARIFIED or RENDERED BUTTER *Samin imfaqis*

Clarified or rendered butter is used especially in rice recipes, baked *kibby* and all pastries. This butter will keep for months. It is more convenient to cook many pounds at one time rather than just a few pounds.

Melt 5 pounds butter in a deep saucepan on low heat for 30 minutes until steam disappears. Set to one side for 30 minutes to let residue settle on bottom of pan. Remove any foam that may still appear on top.

Pour the clear clarified butter in jars and keep in a cool place or store in the refrigerator for future use.

RICE-ORZO DRESSING *Roz ma' sha'reeyee* (this is a popular rice dish that can be served in a platter or in a picturesque ring mold for a dinner party)

2 cups long grain rice
1 teaspoon salt
6 tablespoons clarified butter
1 cup orzo (rosa marina)
4 cups boiling chicken broth
1/2 teaspoon cinnamon

Rinse 2 cups rice thoroughly in warm water and drain. Melt 6 tablespoons butter in pan and add 1 cup orzo. Stir until brown. Add 2 cups rinsed rice, stirring gently about 2 minutes. Add 4 cups boiling chicken broth and 1 teaspoon salt. Mix well and cook on low fire in covered saucepan until water is absorbed, about 25 minutes.

If using a ring mold, brush the mold lightly with oil. Place cooked rice in mold. Cover with aluminum foil. Keep warm until ready to serve. Remove foil. Invert mold onto a round platter. Sprinkle cinnamon on top. A very pretty picture. Garnish with parsley. *Serves 8.* Serve with Marinated Broiled Chicken.

Syrian Party Rice with Orzo SERVING 100

Assemble 4 large cooking vessels
6 cups long grain rice per pan
1-1/2 cups clarified butter per pan
2 cups orzo per pan
10 cups chicken broth or water, boiling per pan
2 tablespoons salt per pan

Rinse 24 cups of rice and drain. In each pan melt 1-1/2 cup butter. Place 2 cups orzo in each pan. Saute until golden brown. Add 6 cups rice to each pan, stirring gently for 3 minutes. Add boiling broth or water and salt. Stir, cover and let cook on medium fire about 30 minutes. (This is great for your large gatherings. Add to the menu green beans, baked *kibby,* salad and *baklawa* and you're sure to have your guests asking for a repeat of this dinner)

ROZ IMFALFEL (This is a traditional way to fix rice for a **Jordanian Mansef Party.**

2 cups long grain rice
4 cups boiling water
6 tablespoons clarified butter
1 teaspoon salt

Rinse and drain rice. Boil the water with 1 teaspoon salt. Add the rice and boil vigorously for 2 minutes. Cover the pan and let simmer for 20 minutes until water is absorbed. Rice will be tender and each grain will stand apart from the other. Rice should not be mushy. Melt 6 tablespoons of butter and pour over all the rice. *Serves 6.*

RICE DRESSING *Hashwa Roz*

- 2 cups long grain rice
- 6 tablespoons clarified butter
- 1/2 cup pine nuts
- 1/2 pound ground beef
- 4 cups boiling water or chicken broth
- 1 teaspoon salt
- 1/4 teaspoon each of cinnamon, allspice, nutmeg and pepper

Rinse rice thoroughly in warm water and drain. Melt butter in cooking vessel. Add 1/2 cup pine nuts. Stir until light brown. Add the ground beef and saute until beef is no longer pink. Add rice and stir gently about 2 minutes. Add the boiling water or chicken broth and the seasonings. Cover and cook on low fire until water is absorbed, about 20 minutes. *Serves 8.*

RICE-GIBLET DRESSING *Roz ma' qiwanis*

- 1 cup rice
- 3 tablespoons rendered butter
- 1/2 pound giblets, chopped
- 1/2 cup pine nuts or english walnuts, blanched and peeled
- 2 cups chicken broth
- 1/2 teaspoon salt

Rinse rice in warm water and drain. Melt butter in pan and add giblets. Saute giblets, then add nuts, stirring until golden. Add rice and stir gently about 2 minutes. Add boiling chicken broth or water and 1/2 teaspoon salt. Cover pan and cook on low fire for 25 minutes. *Serves 4.*

(More rice recipes in the Lenten Section)

Tabouli, yogurt, grape leaves, and shish kabob

Platter of Syrian foods—spinach pies, Fried Kibby, cabbage rolls, Tabouli, Baked Kibby, Labnee, meat pies, and grape leaves

COUSCOUS
National dish of MOROCCO

COUSCOUS *or Maghrabeeyee*

On an invitation by Dr. Victor Miller of Indiana State University to attend a *couscous* dinner party for authors, I returned to their home a week later and watched his wife Lucien make this sumptuous food. They had just returned from Tripoli where Dr. Miller was Geology Chairman at the University of Libya. When friends learned of my interest they presented me with a *couscousiere* for my own *couscous* parties.

 3 cups couscous*
 1/2 cup flour
 1 cup tap water
 2-1/2 pound lamb, cut into large chunks
 1/2 cup butter and 1/2 cup olive oil
    mixed together
 1 large onion, quartered
 4 jalepeno peppers
 1 - 13-1/2 oz. can beef broth
 1 13 oz. can whole tomatoes
 1-1/2 teaspoon turmeric
 1 teaspoon maggi seasoning
 1 tablespoon each of salt and pepper
 4 tablespoons parsley
 1 fresh acorn squash, peeled or fresh
    peeled pumpkin, sliced in wedges
 2 beef boullion cubes
 1-1/2 cup dried chick peas
 5 potatoes, quartered

1. Soak chick peas overnight. Next day, drain.

2. Broth: Salt and pepper the lamb. Heat the butter and oil in bottom of couscousier and saute meat until brown. Add onion. Cook 2 minutes. Add peppers, beef broth, tomatoes, turmeric, and 1 quart hot water. Stir in seasonings and parsley.

3. Mix couscous with 1/2 cup flour. Rub together. Add 1 cup tap water. Rub together until grains separate and do not stick together. Place in top part of couscousier to steam. Seal the rim of the bottom part of couscousier by taking 2 strips of wet cloth (or use dough to seal) and wrap around the rim so that top and bottom fit snugly. This is done so steam does not escape. With wet hands, rub grains gently breaking up any lumps. Cover the pan, check the grains every 10 minutes to separate any lumps. Remove seal of pan and make sure broth does not evaporate. Add more water if needed. Reseal, and simmer for 30 minutes.

4. Remove seal on pan and add squash and pumpkin. Reseal and cook 30 minutes. Then add beef boullion cubes and more seasoning. Add chick peas and potatoes and cook another 15 minutes.

5. Add 1/2 cup butter/oil mixture to couscous and mix together to keep the grains separated.

To serve, place the couscous onto a deep serving dish. Rub in 1/2 cup butter making sure there are no lumps. Pour juice from vegetables and meat directly onto couscous in dish. Layer the vegetables on top of the meat and serve. *Serves 10.*

* **Couscous** - durum semolina wheat grains.

COUSCOUS, fast cooking method (purchase boxes from specialty stores)

    1 cup water   1 teaspoon oil
    Dash of salt   1-1/4 cup fast cooking *couscous*
                                                                                     3 teaspoons butter

In a large saucepan, boil 1 cup of water. Add dash of salt and one teaspoon oil. Remove from heat and sprinkle 1-1/4 cups *Couscous* into the water and stir gently. Cover and let stand for 2 minutes (all the water will be absorbed by the *Couscous*).

Add 2 tablespoons butter or margarine, then return to low heat for 3 minutes, stirring with a fork to separate grains. *Yield: 4 servings.* Serve with steamed vegetables for a hearty meal. For party servings, roast a Turkey and serve with your *Couscous*.

COUSCOUS SALAD IN TOMATO CUPS   Watching your weight? Try this low-fat salad following your aerobics class.

    1 cup chicken stock, boiled   1/3 cup dried mint
    1/4 cup *couscous,* fast cooking   1 green pepper
    3 teaspoons butter   Juice of 1 lemon
    3 green onions, chopped   3 tablespoons olive oil
    6 large tomatoes   1/2 teaspoon salt
    1/2 cup parsley, chopped   1/2 teaspoon pepper

Boil chicken stock. Add a dash of salt and 1 teaspoon oil. Remove from heat and add *couscous,* stirring gently. Cover and let stand 2 minutes. Return to heat, add 3 teaspoons of butter and heat for 3 minutes, stirring to separate grains. Remove from heat; place in large bowl, fluffing with fork. Scoop out tomatoes. Chop inside of tomatoes. Add to *couscous* grains along with onions, parsley, mint, salt, pepper, lemon and oil. Fill the tomato cups. Serve on a luncheon plate lined with lettuce leaves. Garnish the edges of platter with carrot and celery sticks. *Serves 6.*

WHEAT AND KIBBY

Burghul wa Kibby

(Num. 18:12; KI. 5:ll; St. Luke 3:17, Prov. 27:22; Ps. 81:16)

Fallaheen (farmers) sweat in the sun to harvest wheat in the Middle East. After the harvest, baskets of the freshly cut grain are taken to rivers and washed. The wheat is then boiled in pots for hours; later it is spread in the sun to dry and harden. While it is drying, women sort the grain from the chaff. The wheat is ground in a stone mill and the grain kernels are sorted again.

While the men tend to the harvest, women cook in iron cauldrons and make bread flaps from wheat ground by hand between flat stones and baked on iron skillets. Bread made from wheat flour is considered the staff of life. Reverenced highly in the partaking of Holy Communion in the Eastern Orthodox Church, if a piece drops on the floor, it is immediately picked up and kissed in atonement.

This nutty-flavored cracked wheat is sold precooked and packaged in the United States in 3 forms: fine, medium and coarse. The Arabic name for the wheat is *burghul*. The U.S. Department of Agriculture in conjunction with flour-milling companies in the United States has established a more scientific process of manufacturing *burghul* (known also as *bulgur*), but almost the same steps - washing, dehydrating, cooking, drying, and cracking wheat - are used in the United States as in the Middle East.

The fine grain wheat is used in the making of *kibby*, the medium or fine grain for making *tabooley*, and the coarse grain in the tasty boiled dishes found in the entire Middle East.

Another form of wheat is finely ground wheat meal (usually semolina) used by **Egyptian** cooks in the making of their national dish of **couscous.**

Kibby, the national dish of **Syria and Lebanon**, is made from *burghul* along with the meat. Sunday dinner is incomplete without *Kibby neeyee*. While there are many variations of *kibby,* it all starts with the basic Raw Kibby.

Only until recently has the public been made aware of the nutritional values of protein-filled wheat, a health food of the Middle East for centuries.

RAW KIBBY *Kibby neeyee*

2 pounds lean round steak or lean lamb* (ground twice with fine blade)
1 large onion, grated
1 cup fine cracked wheat *burghul*
2 teaspoons salt
1 teaspoon pepper
1/2 cold water

Rinse wheat in cool tap water several times until water is no longer cloudy. Squeeze moisture out of wheat by cupping hands. Add salt and pepper, 1 grated onion, and rub together with palms of both hands. Add the 2 pounds of meat and knead together all ingredients. Add 1/2 cup cold water to soften, and knead again until smooth and moist.

Garnish platter with green onions. In a separate bowl, serve melted clarified butter to spoon over *kibby* for a tasty addition. *Leg of lamb with all fat removed is the best cut for *Kibby*. *Serves 8*. Serve with *Salata*. Be sure to have loaves of thin Syrian bread on hand to wrap *kibby* into the bread. Add some pickled vegetables to the meal, especially pickled turnips.

This PARTY SERVING for Raw Kibby will yield 100 SERVINGS when added to other foods for dinner parties:

    10 pounds lean round steak, ground twice
    7 cups cracked wheat, fine
    1 quart pureed onions (4 large onions)
    2 tablespoons salt
    1-1/2 tablespoons pepper
    1 cup cold water (enough to keep *kibby* a smooth texture).

Follow above method of rinsing wheat, adding ingredients and kneading until *kibby* is smooth and moist. This basic recipe will be used for making football shaped *kibby qras*.

Qras mihshee (Fried Kibby). 1. Rubbing together spices, wheat, meat, and onions. 2. Kneading together all ingredients. 3. Perforating end of football-shaped kibby. 4. Placing filling in perforated end of kibby.

BAKED KIBBY, FOOTBALL SHAPE *Qras mish-wee* *(photo on page 56)*

Raw Kibby recipe
- 1/2 pound ground lamb or beef
- 1/4 cup pine nuts or English walnuts
- 1/2 teaspoon each of cinnamon and salt
- 1/4 teaspoon each of allspice and pepper
- 4 tablespoons butter, melted
- Bowl of ice cold water

Brown lamb in butter. Add nuts and spices. Shape *kibby* by taking a small ball of the mixture and shape like mini-footballs, about 4 inches in length. Using index finger, perforate end of *kibby* at one end, pressing with finger to make inside hollow. Keep pressing inside walls toward palm with finger, slipping it around in palm of hand. Fill the shell with a tablespoon of filling. Close end of *kibby* by rotating in palm of hand, dipping hands in bowl of ice water while shaping.

Place *kibby* side by side in a tray brushed with butter. Brush tops with butter. Bake in preheated oven (450°) until golden brown, approximately 15 minutes, then broil 3 minutes. If you prefer, you can deep-fry to a golden brown. *Yield:* One dozen 4" long *Kibby*.

KIBBY with LABAN and WALNUTS (your guests will love this) Use the same recipe as above with this filling:

Mix together: 1/2 cup Yogurt Cheese, 1/3 cup pomegranate seeds, 1/3 cup chopped English walnuts. You'll find it difficult for you to keep from snacking on these all day long,

KIBBY PATTIES; *Qras miq-lee* (great for picnics)

Raw Kibby recipe. In palm of hand, flatten balls of raw *kibby* until about 1/2 inch thick, 3-1/2 inches in diameter, like hamburgers. Fry in hot oil until brown on both sides. (Make a kibby burger by placing in pocket bread and topping with *salata*.) Serves 8.

LOW CHOLESTEROL KIBBY made with Turkey *Qras il habesh*

- 1-3/4 cup cracked wheat, fine
- 1-1/2 pound ground turkey
- 1 teaspoon each salt and cinnamon
- 1-1/2 teaspoon pepper
- 1 large onion, pureed
- 1/2 cup cold water

Rinse wheat in tap water several times until no longer cloudy. Drain water from wheat. Use same method of mixing together ingredients as in Raw Kibby recipe. Shape into patties like hamburgers. Place on a lightly oiled baking tray and bake in preheated 450° oven until golden brown on bottom, then broil until golden on top. Serve in pita bread topped with salad. (You'll never know that turkey has been substituted for meat).

KIBBY WITH YOGURT-RICE SAUCE *Kibby laban-ee-yee*

Raw kibby recipe

Use same filling as in Baked Kibby football-shape recipe. Saute lamb in butter. Add pine nuts and spices. Make 12 football-shaped *kibby*. Perforate end of *kibby* with index finger, pressing down toward palm of hand to make *kibby* hollow. Put 1 teaspoon filling in each *kibby* and close end. Cook in boiling water to which 1/2 teaspoon salt has been added. Cook for 3 minutes. Reserve water.

YOGURT RICE SAUCE FOR *kibby laban-ee-yee*

5 cups water from cooked *kibby*   **2 quarts yogurt**
1/2 cup rice   **1 egg, beat well**

Cook rice in water from cooked *kibby*. In another saucepan add well-beaten egg to yogurt. Stir well and cook on low fire. Stir constantly until mixture boils. Add rice. Cook 5 more minutes. Place *kibby* in sauce. Serve hot. *Serves 6.* (When your friends find out that you're making this dish, they'll come out in the snow for this winter favorite. Have some red wine on hand and hot Syrian bun-type bread *talamee* .)

KIBBY WITH KISHIK SAUCE *Kibby kishik*

Same ingredients and method as Kibby with Yogurt. This is another tasty sauce for Kibby.

KISHIK SAUCE:
1 onion, diced   1-1/2 cups *kishik*
1/4 cup chopped lamb   5 cups water from cooked kibby
2 tablespoons butter

Brown onion and lamb in butter. Add *kishik* and mix. Cook on low fire about 1 minute. Add water to mixture and stir. As soon as mixture comes to a boil, add *kibby* and cook 2 more minutes. *Serves 6.*

BAKED KIBBY *Kibby bil san-ee-yee*

Raw kibby recipe   1/4 cup pine nuts
Clarified butter   1 teaspoon each cinnamon and allspice
1 pound coarse ground lamb   1-1/2 teaspoon salt
4 tablespoons butter   1 teaspoon pepper
1 medium onion, chopped   Bowl of ice water

Grease a 10"x14" baking pan with clarified butter. Dip hand in water and spread half of Raw Kibby smoothly over bottom of pan., (Procedure of doing this is to form flat patties of kibby and placing them next to each other firmly on bottom of pan with palm of hand) making sure that pan is completely covered. Simmer lamb in butter. Add seasonings and mix. Saute onions and pine nuts in butter and add to meat. Spread this filling evenly over the layer of *kibby* in pan. Cover filling with remaining *kibby,* putting 1 patty at a time next to each other.

Smooth surface well with hands moistened with water. Score in diamond shapes with a knife dipped in cold water. Loosen edges from tray with knife. Pour 1 cup clarified butter on top. Bake in preheated oven (350°) approximately 40 to 45 minutes until a golden brown. The last 20 minutes, place on top shelf of oven. *Serves 10. Yield: 45 cuts.*

Making football-shaped Kibby—recipe on page 54

Baked Kibby

OMELETS

Ijee

A popular breakfast in the Middle East is the omelet which takes only a few minutes to prepare. Similar to the United States' western omelet, the *'ijee* is served with *marquq* (Syrian bread)

EGG OMELET *Ijee*

6 eggs	Salt and pepper
2 tablespoons each of parsley and mint, chopped fine	2 tablespoons flour
4 green onions, minced	4 tablespoons oil

Mix eggs with parsley, mint, onions, salt and pepper. Add flour and mix. Fry in hot oil until golden on both sides. *Serves 8.* (flour gives this omelet a nice full thick texture)

SQUASH-EGG OMELET PATTIES *Ijet koosa*

You'll want to make this immediately after saving the pulp from the squash in Stuffed Squash recipe.

4 eggs, beaten	6 sprigs parsley, chopped
1/2 cup flour	Salt and pepper to taste
1 hot pepper	

Salt the pulp and squeeze out as much of the moisture as possible. Mix together all ingredients and shape into patties. Fry in hot oil until golden on both sides. Serve cold.

NOTE: An excellent sandwich served on *mra-qud*, topped with a slice of tomato, onion and fresh mint.

SQUASH OMELET *Imfarakat koosa*

3 medium-size squash	4 eggs, beaten
1 onion, chopped	Salt and pepper to taste
5 tablespoons butter	

Wash squash and dry thoroughly. Cut in small pieces. Saute onion and squash in butter. Cook on low heat until tender. Add eggs and seasonings. Mix well. Cook 2 minutes. *Serves 6.*

Helen's father

*Michael (Mkhayel) Albert Corey
Ein-el-shara, Syria*

VEGETABLES

Khuthra

We learned at an early age from Dad that sharing with others was one of the greatest rewards of making others happy, especially those in need. He was born in the village of *Ein-el-Shara*, not too far away from *Arne,* near *Jebel al Sheikh* (Mount Haramoon). Dad was known for his compassionate giving ways and was a man with a heart of gold. When he came home from his journey selling linens and oriental rugs around the state of Ohio, his car was always laden with fresh country eggs and bushels of fruit, vegetables and other provender. He immediately went to the homes of those in need and filled their cupboards and tables.

Both Mom and Dad were raised on farmlands in Syria. After a brief courtship in Canton, Ohio, they married and settled down in Canton to be near other cousins who migrated there from Syria. There is a close-knit family relationship that is traditional with Syrians that is still evidenced today.

Blessed with their knowledge of gardening, ours flourished then and now with a myriad of delights from which to choose a meal at any given time... turnips, beets, okra, and the versatile eggplant used in making *Sheikh il mihshee*, a stuffed eggplant that most men prefer to all foods. The garden also produces an abundance of nutritional foods including some giant-size green beans *lubee* that measure some 24 inches long. Those that know about her "green thumb" marvel at Mom being the first to plant fava beans after March 15th (following the first full moon before spring) when the ground is tillable. The *ful* is one of the tastiest of all beans cooked with or without lamb and a hint of *kizbara* (cilentro) in the dish called *ful-eeyee*. Our garden is filled with *koosa* (light green summer squash) and *mulfoof* cabbage to be used as principal dishes once stuffed with rice and meat and cooked to perfection tantalizing anyone's palate.

Near the garden, with the fruits, herbs and vegetables, there is a grape arbor winding around a shelter of trellises that we call our "house of grapes and grape leaves." Hospitality is one of our well-known pleasures, whether offered indoors or out. On a summer afternoon, friends are invited to a *tabooley* party. Picnic tables are set up under the trellised roof of vines and grapes that are within reach of the guests. The tender leaves are used as scoops for eating *tabooley,* the favorite **Syrian-Lebanese** wheat garden salad. The leaves are also used for making *waraq 'inib mihshee* (grape leaf rolls stuffed with *hashwa* , a mixture of chopped lamb, rice and spices).

One of the greatest hobbies you can have is to plant a garden, nurture it and find a great sense of satisfaction when it's harvest-time. And you'll find yourself saying: "God bless the farmers who toil hard to make it possible for the food on our tables." **(Song of Solomon 6:ll)**

FAVA BEANS WITH CILENTRO *Ful-eeyee ma' kizbara*

>   3 tablespoons olive oil
>   10 sprigs fresh cilentro *kizbara*, chopped
>   1 large clove garlic, crushed
>   4 cups fresh fava beans, broken into 3" pieces
>   Salt and pepper
>   1 cup water
>   Lemon wedges

Saute cilentro and garlic in olive oil, stirring for 2 minutes. Add fava beans and saute for another 5 minutes. Then add 1 cup water, salt and pepper. Cover and cook until tender, about 30 minutes. *Serves 4.* Serve with lemon wedges.

FAVA BEANS WITH LAMB *Ful-eeyee ma' lahum ghanum*

>   1/2 pound lamb, cubed
>   Butter
>   1 onion, diced
>   1 clove garlic, chopped
>   1 pound fava beans, cut into 3" pieces
>   1 cup water
>   Salt and pepper to taste

Brown meat in butter. Add onion and garlic and simmer. Add beans and saute 5 more minutes. Add water, salt and pepper. Cook in covered pan on low fire until beans are tender, about 30 minutes. *Serves 4.* (Green beans can be substituted for above recipes.)

CABBAGE ROLLS *Mulfoof mihshee or Yubraq*

>   2 heads cabbage
>   Lamb bones (optional)
>   1 cup canned tomatoes
>   1 teaspoon salt
>   2 cloves garlic, cut in half
>   Juice of 2 lemons

Carve out thick core from center of cabbage. Drop cabbage into salted boiling water, cored end down. Boil a few minutes until leaves are softened. While boiling, loosen each leaf with a long fork, remove and place in a dish to cool. Remove heavy center stems from the leaves. If leaves are extremely large, cut in half. Fill each leaf with 1 teaspoon stuffing and roll in the shape of a cigar. Place lamb bones or cabbage stems on the bottom of kettle. Arrange cabbage rolls on top of bones or stems, alternating in opposite directions. Add tomatoes, salt and garlic. Press down with inverted dish. Add water to reach dish. Cover kettle and cook on medium fire 25 minutes. Add lemon juice and cook 10 minutes more.

STUFFING;
>   1 cup rice, rinsed in water
>   1 pound ground lamb or beef, fat and lean
>   1/2 cup canned tomatoes (optional)
>   1/2 teaspoon cinnamon
>   Salt and pepper to taste

Combine all ingredients and mix well. *Yield:* 56 rolls, serving 8. (about 7 rolls per person)

Cabbage Rolls, PARTY SERVING FOR 50 PEOPLE, 10 rolls per person.

8 large heads of cabbage	10 cloves garlic, cut in half
6 cups canned tomatoes	Juice of 8 lemons
6 teaspoons salt	

STUFFING:

3 cups rice, rinsed in water	2 teaspoons cinnamon
4 pounds ground lamb or beef	Salt and pepper to taste
2 cups canned tomatoes	

Combine all ingredients and mix well. Follow method of preparing as in above recipe. *Yield: 500 rolls.*

SWISS CHARD *Silliq mihshee* (use same method as Cabbage Rolls)

BROCCOLI *Lah-youn*

1 pound broccoli	3 cloves garlic, chopped
6 tablespoons oil	Salt and pepper to taste

Cook the broccoli in boiling salted water and, when tender, remove the broccoli and drain thoroughly. Chop coarsely. Put the oil in a skillet. When hot, add the cloves of garlic. When these begin to brown, add the broccoli and season with salt and pepper. Cook 20 to 30 minutes, stirring occasionally. *Serves 4.*

FRIED CAULIFLOWER *Zahra qar-na-beet*

1 egg, well beaten	1 medium cauliflower
Salt to taste	Juice of 1 lemon (optional)

Steam cauliflower with 1/4 cup water. When tender, remove from water and break off into flowerets. Dip into the well-beaten and salted egg. Fry until golden brown in deep oil. Sprinkle with lemon juice or serve with *taratoor* sauce. *Serves 4.*

CAULIFLOWER WITH TOMATOES AND LAMB *Qarnabeet wa banadoora*

1 cauliflower	1 cup tomato puree
1/2 pound lamb, cubed	1 cup water
Butter	Salt and pepper to taste

Parboil cauliflower. Brown lamb in butter. Add tomato puree and water to lamb and stir. Add parboiled cauliflower and cook until tender. Season. Excellent side dish with rice. *Serves 4.*

STUFFED BAKED EGGPLANT *Sheikh il mihshee - Bantinjan bil saneeyee*

  3 eggplants
  1 15-ounce can tomato sauce, thinned with a little water
  1/4 cup olive oil

Make sure eggplant are dark purple with no bruises. Light colored eggplant tend to be bitter. Trim off the stems. If eggplant are large, cut in quarters lengthwise. If they are small, cut in half. Place cut side down in oiled 9" x 13" baking tray. Bake 15 minutes in preheated 450º oven. Take the baked eggplant and make a slit on one side making sure not to cut all the way through. Stuff each piece with about 2 tablespoons filling. Place stuffed eggplant back in baking tray side by side. Pour tomato sauce over all and bake at 400º for an additional 20 minutes. *Serves 8.*

FILLING *Hashwa* **(Use turkey for a low-cholesterol filling)**

1 pound ground lamb
 (or ground turkey)
Dash allspice, nutmeg, cinnamon
1/2 pound low-fat margarine
1 onion, chopped
1/2 cup pine nuts
(If using turkey, in-crease seasonings to 1 teaspoon each)
Salt and pepper to taste

Saute lamb and onion in margarine. Remove from skillet and brown pine nuts in margarine. Remove from skillet and mix together all ingredients

EGGPLANT STEW *Yukh-net batinjan*

- 1 pound lamb, cubed
- 5 medium eggplant, peeled and cubed
- 1 large onion, chopped
- 3 tablespoons butter
- 1 No. 2 can tomatoes
- Salt and pepper to taste

Boil meat in water for 30 minutes. Fry onion in butter, then add to meat. Add the cubed eggplant, tomatoes and seasonings and cook on medium heat for 30 minutes. *Serves 6-8.*

EGGPLANT AND CHEESE *Batinjan wa joban*

- 1 medium eggplant
- 1 egg, beaten
- 1 teaspoon salt
- 1/4 cup corn oil
- 1/4 pound sharp cheese
- 1 8-ounce can tomato paste
- 4 tablespoons minced onion

Cut eggplant into slices 1/4-inch thick. Dip slices in egg beaten with 1/2 teaspoon salt. Saute in hot oil until brown on both sides. Arrange these slices in shallow baking dish. Place slice of cheese between layers of eggplant and top each stack with a slice of cheese. Thin the tomato paste with water and pour around the stacks. Spread the onion over all adding 1/2 teaspoon salt. Bake in moderately hot oven (350°) for 25 minutes or until cheese is melted. *Serves 6.*

GRAPE LEAF ROLLS *Waraq 'inib mihshee*

Grape leaves prepared in brine can be purchased at Middle Eastern Food stores listed in Shoppers' Guide. Just rinse the leaves thoroughly in cold water, squeeze out moisture, and stuff. Fresh grape leaves are plentiful in early spring and can be found on grape vines in most neighborhoods. Just ask someone of Middle Eastern extraction in your community, and they'll direct you to a multitude of grape vines.

- 50 grape leaves
- 1 teaspoon salt
- Juice of 3 lemons
- 4 lamb bones or 6 chicken wings (optional)

Soak fresh grape leaves in hot water for 15 minutes to soften. Remove from water, squeeze out moisture, and stem each. Place 1 tablespoon stuffing across each leaf, fold end of leaf like an envelope, and roll away from you. Place lamb bone or chicken wings on bottom of pan, and if rhubarb is available, try a few stalks on bottom of pan for a mellow lemony flavor. Arrange stuffed leaves in rows in pan, alternating direction of each row. Sprinkle salt over stuffed leaves. Press leaves down with inverted dish. Add water to reach dish. Cover pan and cook on low fire for 40 minutes until tender. During last 10 minutes of cooking, add lemon juice.

STUFFING:

2/3 cup long grain rice, rinsed in water
1 pound ground lamb or beef, fat
　and lean
3 tablespoons butter
1/2 teaspoon cinnamon
Salt and pepper to taste
3 tablespoons lemon juice

Combine all ingredients, mix well, and set aside. When cooked, serve with lemon wedges. A side dish of yogurt is an excellent accompaniment. *Serves 6.*

GRAPE LEAF ROLLS, **PARTY SERVING FOR 22,** 8 rolls per person

176 vine leaves
3 teaspoons salt
Juice of 6 lemons

STUFFING:
2 cups rice
2-1/2 pounds ground lamb or beef
1/4 pound butter
Salt and pepper

Prepare in same manner as previous recipe for Grape Leaf Rolls

TURKEY STUFFED GRAPE LEAVES *Waraq 'inib ma' habesh*
(Use same method as Grape Leaf Rolls)

STUFFING:
1/3 cup rice, rinsed in water
1 pound turkey, ground
1 teaspoon each of cinnamon, pepper, allspice
4 tablespoons low cholesterol butter

Combine all ingredients, mix well. Place turkey wings on bottom of pan. Arrange stuffed leaves in rows in pan. Continue with above procedure omitting salt. *Yield: enough to stuff 68 grape leaves.* SERVE WITH TURKEY QRAS (Kibby) and Yogurt. **This is a nice change for those watching their cholesterol.**

STUFFED PEPPERS *Fly-flee mihshee*

1 dozen green peppers
1 large can tomato puree
2 cups water

Cut stems off of peppers and set to one side for topping peppers. Remove seeds and membranes, rinsing well.

STUFFING:
- 1 cup rice
- 2 pounds ground beef or lamb
- 1/2 cup canned tomatoes (optional)
- 1 tablespoon cinnamon
- 1 teaspoon salt
- 1/2 teaspoon pepper

Mix together above ingredients. Fill peppers 3/4 full to allow rice to expand. Cap with stems, securing with toothpicks and set peppers in a pan side by side, stems upward. Cover with tomato puree and water and cook on low fire for 40 minutes. *Yield: 12.*

GREEN BEANS *Lu-bee - Fajoom*

- 1 pound green beans
- 1-1/2 pounds lamb chunks
- Butter
- 1 onion, diced
- 1 clove garlic, chopped
- 1 tablespoon salt
- 1 12-ounce can tomatoes
- 2 cups water
- 1/2 teaspoon pepper

Stem beans. Cut in half and rinse in cold water. Saute lamb chunks in butter. Add diced onion and garlic and brown. Add beans and salt. Cover and steam on low fire approximately 45 minutes. Stir occasionally to keep from sticking. Add tomatoes and water even with beans. Correct seasoning. Cook 15 minutes until tender. *Serves 4.*

OKRA *Bay-mee*

- 1 pound okra
- Butter
- 1-1/2 pounds lamb chunks
- 1 cup water
- 1 tablespoon salt
- 2 cloves garlic
- 1 tablespoon coriander (optional)
- 1 11-ounce can tomato sauce
- Juice of 2 lemons

Wash okra and cut off stems. Brown lightly in butter. In separate pan, brown meat lightly in butter. Add water and salt. Cover pan and cook on low fire until meat is tender. Add crushed garlic and coriander to meat and mix. Add okra. Add water even with okra, the tomato sauce and lemon juice. Boil about 5 minutes, then simmer on low heat for 10 more minutes. *Serves 4-5.*

LIMA BEANS AND LAMB *Fasoolya ma' lahum*

- 1 pound lamb, cubed
- 1/4 pound butter
- 2 medium onions, chopped
- 1 clove garlic, crushed
- 1 cup water
- 1 8-ounce can tomato sauce
- 1 teaspoon salt
- 1/2 teaspoon pepper
- 1 teaspoon allspice
- 2 cups frozen lima beans

Saute meat in butter. Add onions and cook until limp. Add garlic, water and tomato sauce along with seasonings. Stir and cover. Cook on low heat for 15 minutes, until meat is tender. Then add lima beans and cook covered for another 10 minutes. *Serves 4-6.* This is a great company dish served on top of Rice-Orzo dressing.

RICE-EGGPLANT INVERTED *Maq-loo-bee*

There are many variations of *maq-loo-bee*...another favorite replaces the eggplant with fried cauliflower.

> **2 medium size eggplant**
> **1 cup orzo***
> **4 tablespoons clarified butter**
> **3 cups long grain rice, rinsed**
> **6 cups water, boiled (or chicken broth)**
>
> **1 teaspoon salt**
> **1 pound ground beef or lamb**
> **3/4 cup pine nuts**
> **1/2 teaspoon pepper**
> **3 tablespoons each butter and oil for frying eggplant**

Peel and slice the eggplant to 1/2 inch thick slices. Salt lightly and set to one side. The salt will remove any bitterness that may be in the eggplant.

Saute orzo in butter in a 2-quart saucepan until golden. Add the rinsed and drained rice. Stir gently for a few minutes. Add boiling water and salt. Cover and simmer for 35 minutes until done.

In separate skillet, saute meat and pine nuts until meat is no longer pink and pine nuts are golden. Stir in seasonings and set to one side.

Saute eggplant slices in the hot butter and oil until golden brown. Place eggplant slices in bottom of a casserole. Add a layer of meat mixture. Then add a layer of cooked rice. Repeat the process ending with the rice layer on top. Cover and bake in a 300° preheated oven for 1/2 hour. Remove from oven; remove cover and let set for 1/2 hour.

To serve unmolded, cover casserole with a flat tray or round serving dish and turn upside down. Let stand a few minutes, then gently lift off dish. The eggplant layer should be on top. *Serves 10.*

*NOTE: If orzo is not available, substitute with broken vermicilli pieces, about 1/2 inches long.

STEAMED SPINACH WITH LEMONS *Sabanigh ma' limoon*

> **2 pounds spinach**
> **Juice of 2 lemons**
> **1 teaspoon salt**
> **1/2 teaspoon pepper**
>
> **6 onions, julienned**
> **1/4 cup olive oil**
> **1/4 cup pine nuts**

Wash spinach well. Remove stalks. Place just enough water in pot to cover spinach. Steam 5 minutes on low heat until spinach is limp. Remove from heat and pour off liquid. Mix in lemon juice. Saute onions in oil until golden brown. Saute pine nuts until golden. Garnish spinach with onions and pine nuts. *Serves 4.*

SPINACH WITH MEAT *Sabanigh ma' lahum*

- 1 medium onion
- 1 clove garlic, minced
- Butter
- 2 cups diced lamb
- 1/2 teaspoon allspice
- 1 teaspoon salt
- 2 cups water
- 1 pound spinach
- Lemon slices

Saute onion and garlic in butter. Add meat and saute until no longer pink. Mix in allspice and salt. Add water, cover kettle and simmer until meat is tender, about 15 minutes. Add spinach and cook on medium heat another 5 minutes until spinach is limp. Garnish with lemon slices. *Serves 4.*

SQUASH WITH YOGURT SAUCE *Koosa ablama*

- 2 dozen small green squash
- 1 teaspoon salt
- 4 tablespoons butter

Core squash. Rinse in water and 1 teaspoon salt. Stuff squash with lamb mixture and close end of each squash with toothpicks. Fry the squash in butter until slightly tender. Remove from skillet and drain off all excess butter. Place squash in pan and set to one side.

FILLING:

- 1 pound lamb, chopped fine
- 1/4 pound butter
- 1 onion, chopped
- Dash of allspice, cinnamon and nutmeg
- Salt and pepper to taste
- 1/2 cup pine nuts

Saute meat in butter. Add onion and stir until golden. Add spices, salt and pepper. Remove from skillet. Saute pine nuts in butter until golden. Mix together all ingredients. Set aside to cool.

SAUCE: Marqeh

- 2 quarts yogurt
- 1 tablespoon cornstarch or beaten egg white
- 1 clove garlic
- 1 teaspoon salt
- 1 tablespoon dried mint

Stir yogurt well. Mix cornstarch with water to make a paste. Add to the yogurt and cook on low fire. Keep stirring until it boils. Crush garlic with salt. Add garlic and mint to the sauce. Pour over squash and cook 40 minutes in a covered pan. *Serves 6.*

STUFFED SQUASH *Koosa mihshee*

Squash can be purchased prepared in brine at Middle Eastern stores listed in Shoppers' Guide. The squash are already cored. Just rinse the squash in cold water, squeeze out moisture, stuff, and cook. If you prefer fresh summer squash, ask someone of Middle Eastern extraction in your community where to locate these small tender squash when in season.

1 dozen green squash, fresh
1 can tomato puree
2 cups water
2 cloves garlic
Dried mint

Core squash. Rinse with cold salted water. Stuff 3/4 of the way full, leaving room for expansion of rice. Place in pan, add tomato puree and water. Add garlic and sprinkle dried mint on top of sauce. Cover and cook on low fire about 35 minutes until tender.

STUFFING:
1 cup rice, rinsed in cold water
1-1/2 pounds ground lamb or beef, fat and lean
1/4 pound melted butter
1/2 cup canned tomatoes (optional)
Salt and pepper to taste

Combine ingredients and mix well. *Serves 6.*

NOTE: Save pulp of squash for *Ijet koosa* - See index.

*Koosa mihshee (Stuffed Squash) 1. Coring squash.
2. Stuffing squash. 3. cooked and ready for eating.*

SQUASH WITH TAHINI-YOGURT *Fatit il Koosa*

An excellent company dish served to Mom and I by Naja Chamoun Homsey of Beirut, Lebanon.

3 rounds of pita bread *kmaj*
1 medium can tomato sauce
1 dozen small squash
1 pound ground lamb
1/2 cup pine nuts
2 tablespoons butter
2 cups yogurt

2 cups tahini sauce
1 clove garlic, crushed
1/4 cup pine nuts
1 teaspoon salt
1/2 teaspoon each of pepper and allspice
1/4 cup English walnuts, broken in pieces

1. Fry pita bread pieces in 1/4 cup butter until crisp. Set to one side.

2. Core squash and set to one side.

3. Saute pine nuts and lamb in 2 tablespoons butter. Mix in seasonings. Stuff squash with this mixture.

4. In separate pan, boil tomato sauce with 1/4 cup water. When it boils, turn down to low heat and drop in the stuffed squash. Cook covered for 30 minutes on low heat until squash are tender.

5. In blender (or food processor) blend together the yogurt and tahini sauce, adding 1 crushed clove of garlic.

6. On bottom of serving tray, place toasted pita bread pieces, next layer the tomato sauce, on top of that the yogurt-tahini sauce. Top with the cooked squash. Sprinkle with the sauteed pine nuts and English walnuts. *Serves 6.* Serve with *Fatoush salad*.

ARTICHOKES, STUFFED *Ardashowki mihshee*

Traditionally known for a role it plays with dips, the artichoke makes a complete meal stuffed with meat and pine nuts, and spreading out the leaves creates a pretty floral picture. Each artichoke, unfilled, contains about 150 calories and is a good source of potassium.

PREPARATION OF 4 ARTICHOKES:

Cut off the stem to make a level base. Pull off the coarse, loose leaves around the base. Lay artichoke on its side and cut one inch across the top and discard. With kitchen shears, trim off the tips of the leaves. Remove the tiny leaves in the center and scrape out the thistle-like leaves, discarding them. Rinse thoroughly, making sure you've removed all the inedible choke. Rub the artichoke thoroughly with oil and drop into a kettle of 2 or 3 inches boiling salted water. Reduce heat, cover and cook 25 minutes until fork can easily pierce the bottom. Drain, and place upside down, drizzling with lemon juice. When cool, spread outer leaves and stuff.

STUFFING:
- 4 tablespoons butter
- 1 pound ground beef
- 1/2 cup pine nuts
- 1-1/2 cups tomato sauce
- 1 teaspoon cinnamon
- 1 teaspoon allspice
- Salt and pepper

In skillet, saute pine nuts until golden. Add the ground beef and cook until brown. Stir in the tomato sauce and seasonings. To spoon in filling, gently press down outer leaves. Spoon stuffing between leaves and fill the center. Cover with foil and bake for 35 minutes. THIS MAKES A COLORFUL CENTERPIECE for the rest of your meal.

NAVY BEANS *Fajoom*

- 1 pound navy beans
- 1 onion chopped
- 1 clove garlic, minced
- 1/2 cup butter
- 1 pound beef or lamb, cubed
- 1 10-ounce can tomato puree
- Salt and pepper to taste

Soak beans overnight. Following day drain and cook in fresh water about 1 hour until tender. Saute chopped onion and garlic in butter. Add chunks of meat, salt and pepper, and brown. Add tomato puree and simmer about 1/2 hour, then add beans and continue to simmer until heated through. *Serves 4-6.*

Grape Leaf Rolls, page 63

PICKLES

Mkhullal and Makboos

Pickling of food is important in Middle Eastern cuisine that is rooted in tradition as ancient as civilization. It's known that Arabic people can prepare eggplant in some 20 different ways. When it comes to pickling, the eggplant is a must along with the pickling of turnips.

We take special care in planting eggplant and harvesting them when they are small, about 4" long. It only takes a few plants to provide a large supply of eggplant. Stuffed with English walnuts, this shiny purple beauty stands out as one of the tastiest additions to a *Maza* table.

When Antiochian Orthodox Churches throughout the country hold their annual Middle Eastern festivals, the public is aware that Middle Eastern cooks are not only artists but hard workers as well. They find eating is an esthetic experience, and the exciting variety keeps them coming back for more. Members of the church pickle some 50 gallons of turnips for days, their beet juice producing a zesty red turnip that compliments *kibby neeyee*.

Our cupboards are filled with pickled vegetables. During harvesting season,, whether from our garden or the nearest farmer's market, we'll be getting the best of the crop so we can prepare these pickles and share them with our guests.

GARLIC EGGPLANT *Batinjan m'khullal or makdoos*

12 small eggplant
1 pound English walnuts, coarsely ground
2 tablespoons salt
12 cloves garlic
Olive oil

Remove stems from eggplant. Wash eggplant removing any grit or dirt. Place in pan filled with water. Press eggplant with an inverted dish until water reaches dish. Simmer for 10 minutes. Eggplant will soften slightly. Remove eggplant and place under cold running water. When cool, dry thoroughly. Slit each eggplant on one side. Hold eggplant in your left hand, and with your right thumb, press down into slit of eggplant until all water is removed. Set aside.

Mix together ground walnuts and salt. In slit end of each eggplant, place 1 tablespoon of walnuts 1 clove garlic. Close the opening by pressing together. Place tightly in jar and cover. The following day turn jar upside down. If any water appears in jar, drain well. Fill jar to halfway mark with olive oil. You will notice that oil will rise in jar for 3 to 4 days. Keep an eye on the jar occasionally to see that oil does not spill over. When oil decreases, add more oil to keep eggplant soaked. Keep jar covered. Eggplant will be ready to eat in about a week.

PICKLED TURNIPS *Lift makboos*

5 pounds turnips
Coarse canning salt
Beets, raw preferable
White vinegar
Garlic
Red hot sauce (optional)

Wash turnips. Trim off stems. If turnips are large, cut in quarter sections. If small, leave whole and cut a slash on 1 side. Fill gallon or quart jars with turnips. Add 2 tablespoons salt to each gallon. (1 tablespoon to a quart jar). Add 2 cups vinegar and 2 cups cool tap water to each gallon until it is full. Add 1 clove garlic, and if you like it hot, add a teaspoon of hot sauce. Add about 5 small raw beets to each gallon. (If raw beets are not available, add canned beets and beet juice).

Close lid. Turn jar upside down for 10 minutes so juices can absorb into one another and beet juice bleeds into liquid. Every day, turn jar upside down. Turnips will be ready in 1 week. (If using quart jars, use equal amounts of vinegar and water, adding 1 clove garlic and 1 tablespoon salt to each jar).

SYRIAN CUCUMBERS, PICKLED *Miq-tha makboos*

The seeds for planting this cucumber come from Syria. The cucumber is sweet, crispy, acid-free containing very small seeds.

5 pounds *miqtha*
1 cup coarse pickling salt
3 quarts hot water
3-1/2 cups white vinegar
4 tablespoons pickling spices
3-1/2 cups sugar
1 quart water
Alum
7 quart jars

Scrub cucumbers thoroughly with water. Dissolve 1 cup salt in 3 quarts hot water. (Do not use iodized salt. It causes pickles to darken). Pour over cucumbers. Let stand overnight. Drain and rinse cucumbers the following day. Combine vinegar, pickling spices, sugar and 1 quart water. Heat to boiling. Place cucumbers in hot sterilized jars. Fill with hot liquid. Place 1 teaspoon powdered alum or 1 lump alum in each jar to retain crispiness. Seal at once. Process in boiling water bath for 10 minutes. Ready for eating in 2 weeks. *Yield: 7 quarts*

CAULIFLOWER, PICKLED *Zahra makboos*

2 pounds cauliflower
1/2 teaspoon pepper
1-1/2 tablespoons marjoram
1 clove garlic
2 sweet red peppers
1/4 cup white vinegar
2 cups salad oil
3 pint jars

Trim cauliflower and separate into flowerets. Cook in boiling water 5 minutes. Drain and pat dry with paper towel. Pack cauliflower into sterilized jars. Sprinkle with pepper, marjoram and add clove of garlic and shreds of red peppers. Shake vinegar and oil together vigorously and pour over cauliflower. Seal and store 4 days before using.

PICKLED MIXED VEGETABLES *Khuthra M-khullal*

1 cauliflower	1 cup water
6 small green tomatoes	1 tablespoon salt
1 cup cocktail onions	1 tablespoon mixed pickling spices
1 quart white vinegar	3 pint jars

Trim cauliflower and separate into flowerets. Cook in boiling salted water for 5 minutes. Drain and pat dry with paper towels. Cut tomatoes in quarters, add cauliflower and cocktail onions, and put into sterilized jars. Boil together vinegar, water, salt and pickling spices. Cool and pour over ingredients in jar. Seal and store 5 days before using.

PICKLED MANGOES, HOT PEPPERS, STUFFED WITH CABBAGE *Fly-flee makboos*

This is one of the most popular appetizers on your *maza* table.

1 dozen small mangoes or peppers	2 tablespoons celery seed
1 head cabbage	1 tablespoon mustard seed (Matt. 13:31,32)
2 tablespoons salt	

Cut tops off mangoes and peppers. Remove seeds. Grate cabbage. Salt heavily and let set for 2 hours. Squeeze out moisture. Mix cabbage with celery seeds and mustard seeds. Stuff peppers with this mixture. Place pepper top on and secure with toothpicks so cabbage will not fall out. Place in wide-mouth jars. Pour liquid over all

LIQUID:
  1 quart white vinegar
  2 cups sugar
  1/2 cup pickling spices

Boil together above ingredients and pour over peppers. These will be ready for eating in 10 days.

PICKLED ONIONS *Bus-il makboos*

- 4 pounds small pickling onions
- 1 gallon water
- 1 pound salt
- 6 medium green peppers, chopped
- 1 4-ounce can pimentos, chopped
- 1 tablespoon dried mint
- 2 quarts white vinegar
- 1/2 teaspoon celery seeds
- 1-1/2 teaspoons dried parsley
- 3 tablespoons peppercorns
- 7 cloves garlic
- 1 teaspoon caraway seeds
- 5 pint jars

Peel onions and place in water and salt. Let stand overnight. Next day rinse onions several times in cold water; drain and cut a slash halfway down from top of each onion. Pack into sterilized jars. Sprinkle the green peppers, pimentos and dried mint on top.

Mix remaining ingredients in separate pan and bring to a boil, then reduce heat and cook slowly 30 minutes. Pour over onions. Seal and store 8 days before using. Give jars a good shake every day before using.

SPICED GRAPES *'Inib m-khullal*

- 3 cups sugar
- 1 cup white vinegar
- 1/2 teaspoon each of cardamon seeds, ginger and cinnamon
- 3/4 teaspoon nutmeg
- 1/4 teaspoon sweet basil
- 4 pounds seedless white grapes
- 6 pint jars

Put sugar, vinegar, spices and basil in a saucepan. Bring to boiling point, then boil 6 more minutes. Remove from heat and let cool. Syrup will be very thick at this point. Set to one side. Wash grapes, pat dry and remove stems. Cut grapes in half lengthwise.

Reheat syrup until small bubbles appear on surface. Add grapes and cook several minutes. Grapes should be tender but not soft. Put in sterilized jars and seal. Let stand 2 days before using . (A tasty relish with meat or fish).

There are a number of ways to prepare and store squash. Any one of these will give an appearance and taste of fresh squash.

FROZEN SQUASH *Koosa imfarez*

Method 1. Wash and dry 2 dozen green summer squash. Core squash. Boil 1 gallon water. Add 1 teaspoon salt and the squash. Blanch on medium heat until water starts to boil. Remove squash immediately and set aside to cool. Wrap by half dozens in plastic bags and freeze. When ready to use, remove squash from freezer, stuff, and cook as in recipe for Stuffed Squash.

Method 2. Prepare squash as in Stuffed Squash recipe. Fill with rice-meat mixture. Cook for 15 minutes. Remove from pan and cool. Freeze. When ready to use, follow recipe for cooking Stuffed Squash, minus 15 minutes cooking time.

CANNED SQUASH *Koosa makboos*

Method 1. Core green squash. Place 1/2 teaspoon salt in opening of each squash. Store in covered jar and place in a cool room. When ready to use, rinse thoroughly with cold water. Follow recipe for Stuffed Squash.

Method 2. *Koosa makboos*

1 dozen small green squash	3/4 cup cider vinegar
2 quarts water	3 tablespoons canning salt

Mix together the water, vinegar, and salt. Place in kettle and let come to a boil. Core squash and drop in boiling water solution. Cover and boil about 8 minutes until squash are pliable. Remove from solution and place in sterilized jars. Pour hot solution in each jar, covering squash completely. Seal tightly.

CANNED GRAPE LEAVES *Waraq 'inib makboos; waraq 'areesh; or waraq dawalee*

Waraq 'inib denotes grape leaves that are picked from vines bearing grapes. *Waraq 'areesh or waraq dawalee* denotes vine leaves that are used. The leaves should be gathered when they are young and tender.

Method 1. Wash the leaves thoroughly, remove stems, and arrange in stacks of 10 or 15 leaves, each face up. Roll up into rolls, tie with string and set aside. In a kettle bring to a boil 2 quarts of water and 1/2 cup of salt. Drop bundles into the boiling water; remove 1 at a time after a few minutes. Cool slightly and pack tightly in sterilized pint jars. Pour the boiling water to the top and seal immediately.

Method 2. Place fresh dry leaves 1 at a time in crock, sprinkling salt on each leaf. Cover crock and store. When ready to use, rinse each leaf thoroughly with cold water to remove salt.

Method 3. Freeze the leaves, stacking 50 or 100 at a time. Wrap in freezing paper. When ready to use, drop in boiling water to soften. Stem and proceed to stuff.

BREADS AND PIES

Khobaz wa Fatayer

"Breaking bread" is the most symbolic phrase applied in the every day life of Middle Eastern people.

The Syrian's daily conversation and habits are essentially biblical; they find the blessing of peace and security in "breaking bread" together and with visitors. Bread is often referred to in the Bible; "bread and salt" .."bread and wine".."Christ the bread of life". **(John 6:32-35)**

More popularly known in America as Pita Bread, this bread has been made over iron cauldrons in the Middle East for centuries, and is known as *Mra-qud or Kmaj* (pocket bread). Eliminating the need of a plate and fork, Arabs for hundreds of years traveled in caravans carrying their *mraqud* and filled them with a variety of foods such as *lahum mishwee, falafel, labanee,* and the many foods listed in the appetizer section.

Khobaz arabee, also known as *marquq*, is almost tissue thin. We marveled at Mom as we watched her bake bread, almost tissue-thin, rolling and flapping the dough around from one arm to another and baking it on the floor of the oven. It was nothing for her to use 25 pounds of flour for making the dough at one time. A similar bread is the **Armenian** *lavish*. However, the *marquq* is softened with water, once baked, and eaten with morsels of food wrapped in each torn off section. There are so many types of breads that are offered that extend into the making of pies or tarts known as *Fatayer* by the **Syrians** and *Sanbusiks* by the **Lebanese.** And the sweet bread of *Ka'ick* filled with anise seeds is always included in the breaking of the lenten fast and served with Easter meals.

The making of **Arabic** bread is a ritual. We were always taught to make the sign of the Cross on the dough before setting it to one side for the first rising. And so meaningful said in Arabic do these words apply: *"Ahjuntak wa ta'ibt feek, Ya Soo' il Maseeh, a-hut feek"* asking the Lord to bless this dough.

SYRIAN BREAD (round thin loaves) *Khobaz 'arabee or Marquq*

**1 cake yeast or 1 package dry yeast
5 pounds flour
2 tablespoons salt
1 tablespoon oil
About 6 cups warm water
1 cup fine yellow corn meal
1 cup flour**

Dissolve yeast in 1 cup warm water. Add the salt and oil to the dissolved yeast and mix well.

In a large mixing bowl, place the 5 pounds of flour. Pour the yeast mixture to the side of bowl and 5 or 6 cups warm water and start blending in with the flour, mixing and kneading well, turning over many times until smooth, at least 10 to 15 minutes. Cover with a dry cloth and plastic and set in a warm place about 1-1/2 to 2 hours until dough rises. Cut in sections the size of an orange and roll between cupped hands. Cover again with dry cloth and plastic and allow to rise for 30 minutes. Preheat oven to 450°.

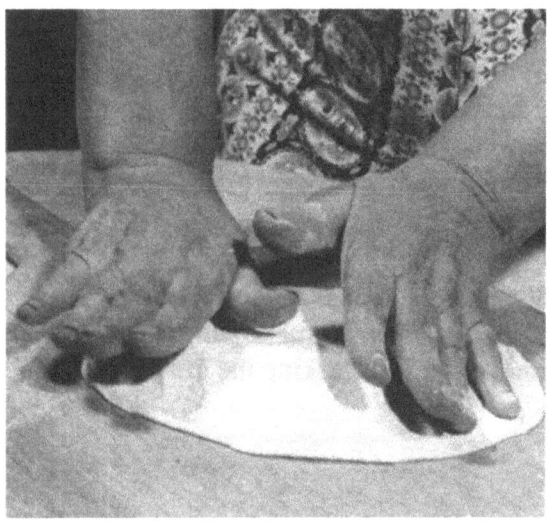
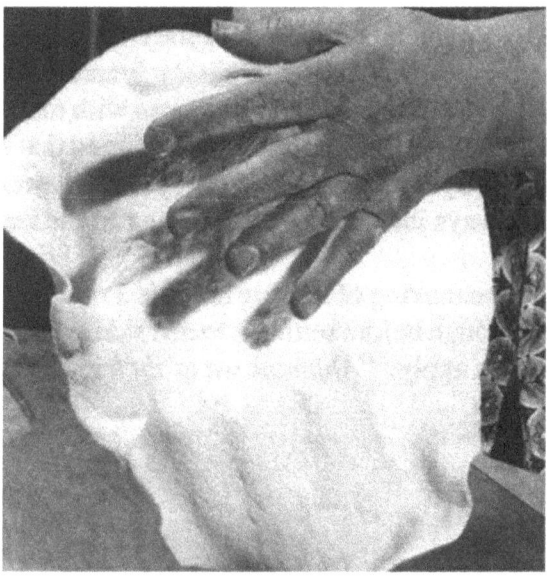

Mix corn meal with 1 cup flour. Dip each piece of dough in corn-meal-flour mixture. Flatten dough and spread with palm of hand to size of pancake (make 12 at a time). Set aside and keep covered with dry cloth and plastic. Then, taking one at a time, spread each piece until you can flap it from one hand to another, and then roll it from one arm to another until it becomes as thin as wrapping paper.

Place dough on lightly floured wooden board with handle. Dough will slide easily from board onto

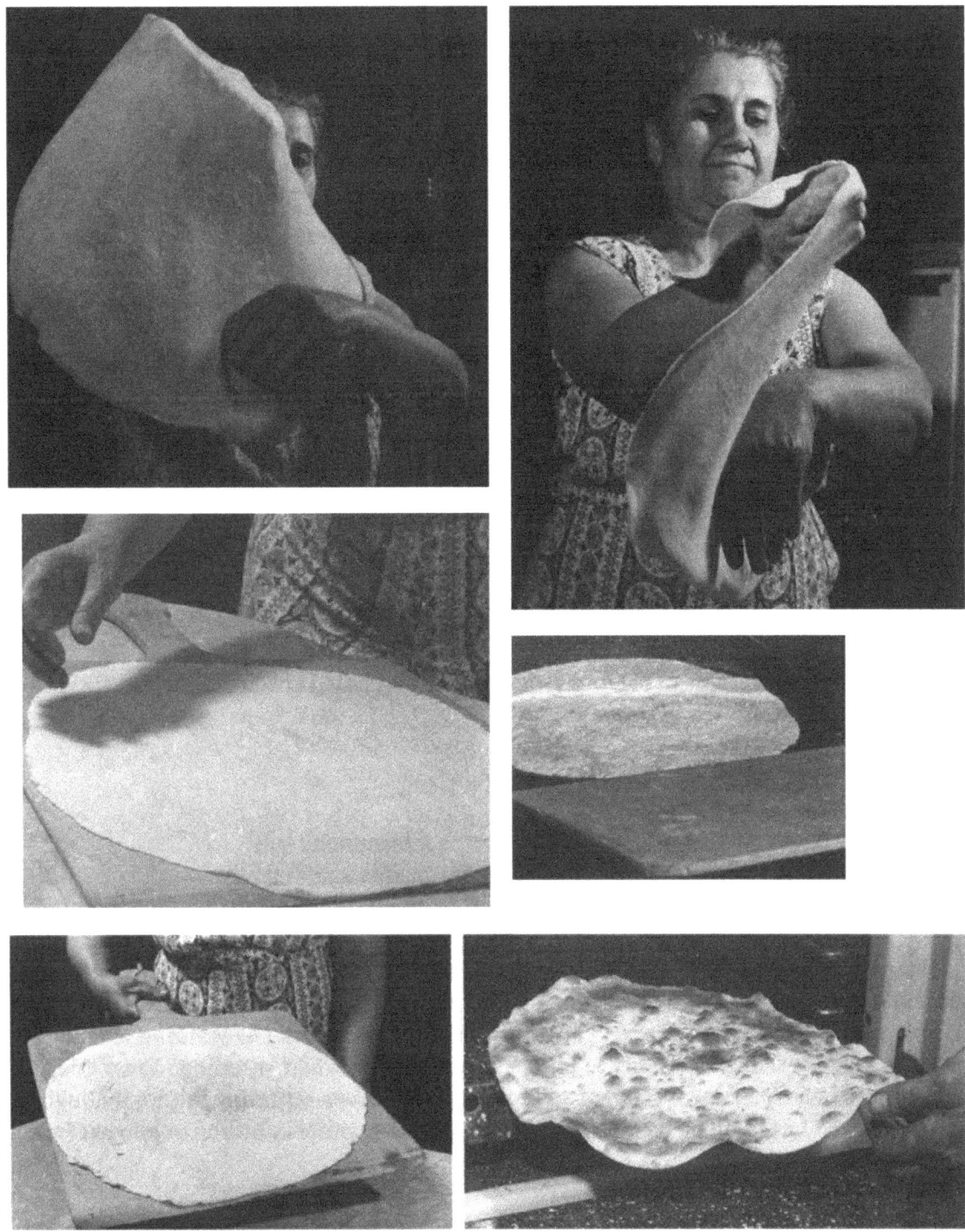

floor of oven. Bake in hot oven (450°) approximately 15 seconds until lightly browned, then place under broiler for a few seconds.

As each loaf is baked, pile one on top of another on table. When baking is completely finished, sprinkle each loaf with water and spread out on table until soft enough to fold (approximately 6 hours). Fold into triangles. Place in plastic bags and store in refrigerator for immediate use. Bread can be frozen in plastic bags (12 loaves to a bag). *Yield: 2 dozen loaves.* (NOTE: Boards can be purchased at Middle Eastern food stores listed in Shoppers' Guide.)

SYRIAN BREAD (round bun type) *Talamee*

2 packages dry yeast	**1 teaspoon of sugar**
5 pounds flour	**2 teaspoons of salt**
1 tablespoon crushed *mahleb* (optional)	**1/4 cup oil**
	Approximately 6 cups warm water

Dissolve yeast in 1/4 cup warm water. Put flour, mahleb, sugar, salt and oil in large mixing bowl. Add dissolved yeast and warm water. Mix well and knead, turning over until smooth, 5 to 10 minutes. Cover with cloth and plastic and set in warm place about 45 minutes to 1 hour until dough doubles in size. Cut into sections, about the size of a grapefruit. Roll between cupped hands until smooth. Cover and allow to rise about 30 minutes.

Preheat oven to 450°. Flatten each ball of dough to 1/4 inch thickness. Brush oil on baking pan and place dough on pan. Bake on lowest shelf of oven until bottoms become light brown and then place under broiler a few seconds until top of bread is lightly browned. *Yield: 12 Talamee.*

NOTE; Mahleb (kernels of black cherries) can be purchased at Middle Eastern food stores listed in Shoppers' Guide.

POCKET BREAD (Pita) *Mraqud or Kmaj*

6 cups flour	**2 teaspoons salt**
1 package dry yeast or 1 cake fresh yeast	**2 cups warm water**
1 teaspoon sugar	**2 tablespoons oil**

Place flour in large mixing bowl. Dissolve yeast in 1/2 cup warm water. Add the sugar and let set until it proofs, about 3 minutes. Mix it together with the oil, salt and 2 cups warm water, Pour it to the side of the bowl and start blending with the flour. Knead dough for at least 10 minutes, dipping hands in warm water occasionally to form a smooth dough while kneading. Press dough down by heel of your hand, pushing it forward and folding back. Keep repeating this until dough is smooth and elastic. (If kneading on board, sprinkle on more flour while kneading to prevent from sticking to the board).

Shape dough into a ball and place in a lightly oiled warm bowl, turning dough over to coat surface with oil. Cover loosely with cloth and set in a warm place for 1-1/2 hours until double in size. Punch down dough and form into 2 dozen balls, the size of oranges. Cover with cloth and plastic and let rest for 20 minutes.

On lightly floured board, roll dough with rolling pin to about 6 inches in diameter and 1/4 inch thick (or flatten with palm of your hand). Place on cloth and cover. Rest for one hour. Preheat oven to 500°. Preheat baking sheet. Lay dough on the ungreased sheet. Bake for approximately 7 minutes. Broil 10 seconds. Remove from oven and brush with butter or oil. The dough will puff up and have a pocket inside. *Yield: 2 dozen.*

ANISE BREAD *Ka'ick* *(photo on page 86)*

A tourist need not search for refreshments and snacks in the bazaars of Damascus. Peddlers with little carts full of glowing charcoal stand on street corners and roast corn on the cob and chestnuts. One favorite between-meal snacks is *Ka'ick*, a round-shaped bread containing anise seeds; the bread is sweetened with a tasty syrup.

7-8 cups flour
2 cups sugar
1 teaspoon salt
3 teaspoons mahleb, crushed
4 tablespoons anise seed

1/4 teaspoon nutmeg
1-1/2 cups milk
1 pound clarified butter
2 tablespoons yeast
2 eggs, room temperature (beat slightly)

Mix together flour, sugar, salt, mahleb, anise seed and nutmeg. Heat milk and butter to lukewarm. While warming up the milk and butter, proof the yeast with .1 teaspoon sugar in 1/4 cup warm water. Pour liquid and yeast mixture in with the flour mixture. Add eggs and knead well until dough no longer sticks to work surface (adding a little flour at a time until it no longer sticks). It should be soft and pliable and especially warm. Work fast while kneading. Cover and let rest 1 hour until dough rises or is doubled. Cut in small pieces 3 inches in diameter. Cover with plastic and cloth. Preheat oven to 350º. Place in dry baking tray, making a design on top with a fork. Bake until bottoms are golden brown, approximately 15 minutes. (Since ovens vary, check the bottoms after 10 minutes so they do not burn). Place under broiler a few seconds until tops are light brown. Take out when golden. *Yield: approximately 50.*

SYRUP FOR ANISE BREAD *Qatir lil Ka'ick*

1 cup half and half cream
1 cup sugar

4 tablespoons butter
1 teaspoon orange blossom water

Combine all ingredients and boil 2 minutes. Place in bowl. Dip each bread in the syrup.

PARTY RECIPE FOR 100 KA'ICK

5 pounds flour plus 1/2 cup
3 tablespoons dry yeast
1 quart milk
1-1/2 teaspoons each, salt and nutmeg

3 cups sugar
2 pounds clarified butter
5 tablespoons anise seed
4 tablespoons mahleb, crushed

Use same procedure as above.

Fatayer - Sfeeha - Lahum bi Ajeen

#1. Maheeba kneading dough

#2. Placing filling on dough patties

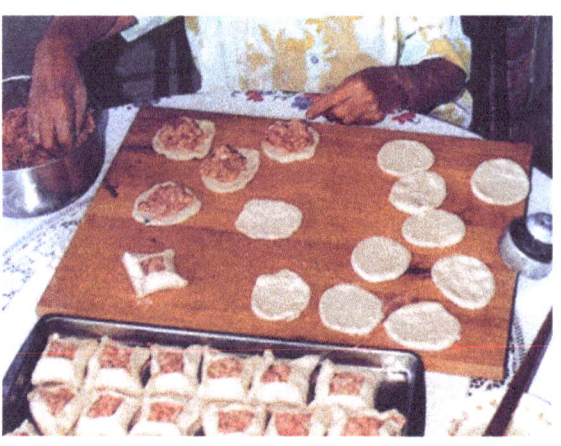

#3. Assortment of Fatayer. Meat Yogurt Spinach pies

BASIC DOUGH FOR PIES *Ajeen il fatayer - lahum bi ajeen*

2 pounds all-purpose flour
1/4 cup oil
1 package dry yeast

1 tablespoon sugar
1 tablespoon salt
About 2-1/2 cups warm water

Dissolve yeast and sugar in 1/4 cup warm water 3 minutes to proof yeast. Put flour in a large mixing bowl. Mix in salt. Make a well in center. Add dissolved yeast and 2-1/2 cups warm water. Mix thoroughly and knead well about 10 minutes, turning over many times until smooth. Dip hands in warm water occasionally while kneading to form a smooth elastic dough. Form dough into a large ball, cover with cloth and plastic and let rest in a warm place until dough rises, approximately 1-1/2 hours. Cut dough in sections to form 3 or 4 round balls. Cover again and let dough rest an additional half hour. While dough is resting, prepare filling. Use any of the various fillings on following pages and shape either in triangles, like turnovers, or fold over on edges, leaving center open. *Yield: enough dough for 3 dozen pies.*

NOTE: If you are in a hurry, use cans of the biscuits found in dairy cases at your grocer's. Spread filling on the biscuit dough and bake according to instructions that follow.

MEAT PIES *Sfeeha*

Sfeeha—open-faced meat pies and triangular-shaped yogurt and spinach pies

Basic pie dough
2 pounds ground chuck or lamb, fat and lean (do not precook)
4 onions, chopped fine
1/2 cup yogurt (or juice of 3 lemons)
1/2 cup pine nuts, sauteed lightly in butter
Salt and pepper to taste

Combine meat, onions, lemon juice, nuts and seasonings. Roll dough about 1/8" thick on lightly floured board. Cut into 3" or 4" rounds. Place filling on surface of dough. Pinch four corners of dough to form tart, leaving center open, or shape into a triangle, pinching together edges of dough. Arrange pies on an oiled baking tray and bake in preheated oven (450°) for 15 minutes until bottoms are lightly browned; then broil a minute or two until tops are lightly browned. Serve hot or cold. Serve with cucumber-yogurt salad. *Yield: 3 dozen.*

(The **Armenians** make a similar meat pie called *Lahum adjoun*. Their filling is tasty with the addition of chopped parsley, tomatoes, thyme, and chopped green peppers and a little lemon to the meat).

Khobaz Smeek Thick bodied skillet bread *(this is a fast and easy to make bread)*

2 pounds all-purpose flour	**1 teaspoon sugar**
3 tablespoons oil	**1 teaspoon salt**
1 package dry yeast	**About 2 or more cups water**
Iron skillet	

Dissolve yeast with sugar in 1/4 cup warm water, letting stand for 3 minutes to proof yeast. Put flour in large mixing bowl. Mix in salt. Make a well in center. Add dissolved yeast and warm water. Mix thoroughly and knead well about 10 minutes to form a smooth elastic dough. Form dough into one large ball. Cover and let rest in a warm place until dough rises, approximately 1 hour. Preheat oven to 350º. Place dough in skillet. Bake approximately 25 minutes until brown on bottom. Last 10 minutes place on top shelf. Remove from oven and let cool before removing from skillet. *(Slice this bread for a great tasting French toast)*

POTATO PIES *Fatayer batata (make this without the meat and you have nice lenten pie)*

Basic pie dough, pg. 82	**1 large onion, grated**
5 pounds potatoes	**Salt and pepper to taste**
1 pound ground beef (optional)	**Clarified butter**
1/4 pound butter	

Shred potatoes. Add pinch of salt to draw moisture from potatoes. Saute beef in butter. Grate the onion. Squeeze all moisture from potatoes. Combine the beef, onion and potatoes and season with salt and pepper. Place on dough patties and close into triangular shape. Fry in clarified butter, 2 minutes on both sides. Serve hot or cold. *Yield: 3 dozen pies.*
Note: *These can also be baked. Brush tray lightly with oil. Bake in preheated 400º oven for 15 minutes until light brown on bottom. Broil a half minute until tops are golden.*

PECAN CRUSTED CHEESE PIES *Fatayer jowz ma'joban - (photo on page 86)*

Basic pie dough, pg. 82	**4 oz. Mozzarella cheese**
4 oz. Roquefort cheese	**2/3 cup pecan halves**
4 oz. Fontina cheese	**4 tablespoons olive oil**
4 oz. Cheddar cheese	

Preheat oven to 400º. Shape dough into 3 to 4 inch rounds. Brush each round with oil. Layer cheeses on top of dough and top with pecans. Spray baking tray with oil and arrange pies on tray. Bake 12-15 minutes until crust is brown. *Yield: 8 pies. (you can also add any cheese you have on hand)*

YOGURT PIES *Fatayer laban ma' qawarma*

Basic pie dough	2 cups Yogurt Cheese
1/4 pound ground beef	1 onion, chopped
3 tablespoons butter	

Saute beef in butter. Mix with Yogurt Cheese and onion. Place on dough patties and close into triangular shape. Arrange pies on oiled baking tray and bake in moderate oven (350°) for 15 minutes, until bottoms are lightly browned. Brown tops lightly under broiler. *Yield: 3 dozen pies.*

PARTY SERVING FOR 80 YOGURT PIES

5 pounds flour	1 teaspoon salt
2 packages dry yeast	6 cups warm water
1 tablespoon sugar	1/4 cup corn oil

(use same method of making dough as above)

FILLING FOR 80 PIES:

Mix together:

1-1/2 gallons yogurt cheese	1 teaspoon pepper
3 large onions, chopped	1 tablespoon butter
1 tablespoon salt	

YOGURT-MINT PIES *Fatayer laban ma' na'na* *

Basic pie dough	1 tablespoon butter
2 eggs	1 tablespoon dried mint
2 cups Yogurt Cheese	1 small onion, chopped

Beat eggs lightly. Add Yogurt Cheese, butter, mint and onion. Place on dough patties and close in triangular shape. Arrange pies on oiled baking tray and bake in preheated moderate oven (450°) for 15 minutes until bottoms are lightly browned. Place under broiler until tops are lightly browned. *Yield: 3 dozen pies.*

*NOTE: For a variation, mix an 8 oz. package of cream cheese (room temperature) with the yogurt cheese.

FATAYER KISHIK *(Kishik is a mixture of yogurt and wheat blend together)*

Basic yeast dough for pies (page 82)
1/2 cup kishik
1/2 cup yogurt
1/2 cup water
1 small onion
1 teaspoon pepper
1 teaspoon butter

Combine ingredients and place on 3" dough rounds. Close into triangular shape. Oil baking tray lightly and bake in preheated 400º oven for 15 minutes. Broil 1 minutes until golden. *Yield: 1 dozen.*

CHEESE PIES *Fatayer Joban* **Make your own calzones out of these.**

Basic yeast dough for pies (page 82)
1 pound sharp cheddar cheese, grated
1 small onion, chopped
1 small hot pepper, chopped
1 tablespoon olive oil
Mix in some hot pepper cheese if you like

Mix together above ingredients. Cut dough into 2 inch rounds. Place mixture on dough and bake in a lightly greased baking tray in preheated 400º oven for 15 minutes until bottoms are lightly browned. *Note: Use whatever cheeses you have on hand and blend them together for great tasting cheese pies. Yield: 8 pies.*

For Calzones, fill the dough, seal edges with water to keep cheese sealed in and fold into crescent shapes. Bake as above.

Anise Bread—Ka'ick
—recipe on page 81.

BEVERAGES

Mushroob

Helen serves her guests Arabic coffee

Tray of Bird's Nests and Finger Pastries

TURKISH - ARAB COFFEE *Qahweh*

Turkish and Arab coffee are both served black in demitasse cups. The coffee is served in brass pots; some pots have long handles and others have long curved spouts resembling a pelican's beak.

Coffee beans are roasted in an open iron ladle until almost burned and then pounded in a mortar to a coarse powder. This rich pulverized coffee can be purchased from Middle Eastern food stores listed in the Shoppers' Guide, or you can use pulverized coffee purchased from your supermarket. The coffee is to be sipped slowly. Thick grounds remain in the bottom of the cup and for a fun evening are used to read fortunes.

A legend about the discovery of coffee was told in Abyssinia, where the berry grew wild. Noticing that his flock of sheep became unusually perky after munching on coffee shrubs, a shepherd partook of the shrubs and was so delighted that he spread word of his discovery around the country. Since then, the practice of drinking coffee has spread all over the world. It has been said that Mohammed, after prohibiting wine, named this invigorating drink *Qahweh*, an expression meaning the **"wine of Araby"**.

Our pelican beak coffee server sits on our bronze arabic inscribed tray on our coffee table ready to serve our guests at the end of an evening as they listen to Mom's endless stories bringing the pages of the Holy Bible alive.

The making of *Qahweh*

2 cups boiling water
1 teaspoon sugar

2 tablespoons Turkish coffee (or pulverized coffee)
2 cardamon pods

Bring water to a boil in a brass coffeepot. Add sugar, then gradually add coffee, stirring until mixture comes to a boil and is frothy. Add cardamon. Remove pot from the fire until froth has receded, then replace pot on brisk fire. Repeat this procedure 3 times. Coffee will rise fast to the top of the pot. The procedure of removing the pot from the fire is repeated 3 times so that coffee will not boil over the side of the pot. As the froth forms, spoon a little into each cup. The froth will rise to the top when coffee is poured into the cup. *Yield: 6 demitasses.*

PUNCH *Shraab*

Almost every known variety of fruit grows in **Syria** and **Lebanon** and **Egypt.** A mixture of fruit juices, boiled together, makes up a drink called *shraab,* a liquid form of sherbet. Orange, pomegranate, strawberry, lemon, raisin, and rose water juices are boiled together with sugar until clear, 1 cup juice to 1/2 cup sugar; the mixture is bottled and put away for future use. To serve, dilute *shraab* with water and ice.

Vendors with portable equipment serve this delicious drink to customers in the streets.

MULBERRY DRINK *Sharbat il toot*

Gathering mulberries every morning was a ritual for us as our bush produced the largest purple-black mulberries ever seen. We had an orchard of trees that included bing cherries, apricots, pears, apples, and quince bushes. The mulberries make for the most refreshing summer drink and we keep the thick liquid on hand to serve to our guests.

Extract the juice of ripe mulberries by placing them in a cheesecloth bag and squeeze tightly. Then place in a container and mash them with a wooden spoon, straining and measuring. For each cup of juice add 2 cups of sugar and 1 tablespoon lemon juice. Boil slowly, stirring constantly. Then simmer until the liquid thickens and coats the back of the spoon. Spoon off any froth rising to the surface. When cool, pour into sterilized bottles. This will be quite thick. When serving, put 1 tablespoon in each glass of ice water and stir.

CINNAMON TEA *Shy ma' qirfee*

To 1 pint boiling water, use 3 teaspoons tea. Let the tea steep in the boiling water for 2 to 5 minutes, according to your taste in strength and flavor. Strain off tea into another hot pot. Serve with lemon wedges and a stick of cinnamon. *Serves 2.*

ANISE TEA *Shy ma' yansoon*

Place 1 teaspoon anise seeds in 2 cups boiling water. Let steep for 10 minutes. Strain and add the anise liquid to 2 cups tea. Garnish tea with chopped English walnuts. *Serves 4.*

SPICE DRINK *Finjan qirfee or Miqlee*
The aroma from the anise seeds will permeate throughout your home and have your guests wondering what is in this wonderful drink.

4 cups water   1 **tablespoon anise seeds**
2 cinnamon sticks   **Sugar**
2 whole cloves   **Almonds or walnuts**
2 ginger roots, cracked

Add spices to water and boil until water turns dark. To serve, add sugar and an almond or walnut to each cup. (This is a healthful drink and traditionally is served to visitors of a new-born baby). *Serves 4.*

NOTE: Double the amount and keep adding water the following day, allowing flavors to intermingle. An exceptionally good winter drink. It gets better each day.

HELEN's SUN TEA (keep a couple of gallons on hand if you're expecting guests.. let the sun do the work)

1 gallon water   **6 cinnamon sticks**
4 tea bags, orange pekoe   **6 large sprigs fresh mint**

Drop tea bags, cinnamon and mint in water. Cover top of jar with plastic. Set in sun. Let flavors intermix for 3 hours.

APRICOT DRINK *Sharbat Qamardeen*

This drink is made from sheets of dried, pressed apricots that are chopped and pureed with water.

It is quite a thick but tasty and healthy drink. *(Qamardeen can be purchased from Middle Eastern specialty stores).*

SYRIAN-LEBANESE LEMONADE *Limoonatha*

4 tall glasses
Juice of 3 lemons
Cold water
4 tablespoons sugar
Few drops of rose-water
Ice cubes

Squeeze lemon juice into a pitcher. Add 4 large glasses of water, sugar and rose-water. Stir with wooden spoon until sugar dissolves. Pour into glasses and add ice cubes. Garnish with a fresh mint sprig. *Yield: 4 servings. (Note: try one drop of rose-water and taste before adding the second drop - this can be over-powering if too much is added).*

Rose Petal drink: Cousin *Shafeeka* in Syria boils rose petals, using only fresh, young petals that are not bruised and have not been exposed to chemicals. Place 4 cups water in saucepan and add 1 cup washed petals. Cover and boil 5 minutes. Petals will discolor. Strain into tea cups and add honey and rose-water. *(Rose water is distilled from rose petals, especially the petals of the* **pink damask rose** *).*

ANISE-FLAVORED LIQUEUR *Araq*

Araq, an anise liqueur is made from the residue of pressed grapes. Great quantities of grapes are consumed yearly in the distillation of this strong spirit. Flavored with anise oil and gum mastic, it looks like water or gin. When a few drops of water are added, it becomes milky like pernod. Unlike European and American aperitifs, *araq* is not poured over ice; ice is added to the *araq*. It should not be mixed with any other beverage.

Such delicacies as *Kibby, Baba ghanouj* and *Batinjan makdoos* may be topped off with a snifter of *araq*. One has only to ask a liquor dealer in America where he can purchase *Araq,* also known as anisette.

WINE *Nbeeth*

Mom and Dad grew up on land surrounded by grape vineyards. Families gathered the grapes and took them to the *ma'sara* (squeezing area) where juices of the grapes were boiled. The longer the juice boiled, it produced a sweeter wine.

From Biblical times, wine has been known to aid in a person's health. **"Drink no longer water, but use a little wine for thy stomach's sake". (I Timothy 5:23).**

CANDIED FRUITS AND PRESERVES

Fa-wa-kee Ma'qood wa Mou-rubba

In the subtropical climate of Syria and Lebanon, the land bears abundant olives, grapes, and figs. The fields are dotted with dense, shady orange groves. On the lower levels stand beautiful summer houses, verdant with gardens and mulberry trees.

Near **Damascus** there is a picturesque spot with fruit trees and sparkling streams called the Goota. The Goota is famous for its apricots. And at the nearby village of **Arne** where my mother was born there is an abundance of apricots near more glistening streams of water. These apricots are sometimes pressed and dried and sold in thin sheets called *Qamardeen* (known in the United States as apricot dried fruit leather).

Safarjel (quince) and colorful *raman* (pomegranate) trees are widely grown in **Palestine** and throughout **Syria**. The trees are seen wherever there are gardens by running water. The pomegranate is filled with small seeds containing a tangy and sweet juice. The cultivation of this oldest fruit known to civilization also encircled the Mediterranean, throughout **Arabia, India and Asia**. The colorful juicy seeds are used to garnish platters filled with many Arabic foods and in fish and rice-dressings.

One of the popular candied fruits is the pear. It is well worth the effort to prepare *Injas ma'qood* (Candied pears) - especially when your guests wonder what this delicious sweet morsel is and ask for the recipe.

CANDIED PEARS *Injas ma'qood*

- 5 pounds pears
- 1 pound sugar
- Ginger root (whole)
- 3 cinnamon sticks
- 1 cardamon
- 3 lemon skins

Peel pears and cut in quarters. Combine pears, sugar, ginger, cinnamon sticks, and cardamon and soak overnight. Following day bring all to boil. Add skins only of lemons. Do not stir. Skim. When thick, remove from fire. Cool and store in jars. (Quinces, peaches, apricots, and plums may be candied in the same way).

SUGARED PEARS *Injas ma' sikkar*

5 pounds pears	3 cinnamon sticks
1/2 pound sugar	Juice of 1/2 lemon
Ginger root (whole)	*Miskee* (gum mastic)
1 cardamon	1 cup sugar

Slice pears into strips and combine with 1/2 pound sugar, ginger, cardamon, and cinnamon sticks. Set overnight. Add lemon juice the following day. Boil, then remove from fire and strain through colander to remove syrup. When cool, lay pear strips on a cloth. Allow to dry overnight. Pound gum mastic and mix with 1 cup sugar. Dip each piece of pear strip in sugar-gum mastic mixture and again set overnight. Cover with wax paper until ready to serve.

SUGARED APRICOTS *Inqoo' mish-mish*

1 pound dried apricots	1 cup granulated sugar
1/2 cup water	1/4 cup blanched almonds

Grind dried apricots. Place in kettle and add water. Cover and simmer until apricots thicken. Add 1/2 cup sugar and cook 10 minutes longer. Cool. Roll into small balls and flatten to about 1/2 inch thick. Place blanched almond in center of each and then dip in remaining 1/2 cup sugar, covering both sides. Cover with wax paper until ready to serve.

CANDIED DATES *Uj-wee*

1 package dates	Almonds
Granulated sugar	

Remove pits from dates. Stuff each with an almond. Press opening to close. Roll in sugar.

SYRUPED EGGPLANT *Batinjan ma'qood*

12 small eggplant (size of lemons)	1 clove
2 cups water	Juice of 1 lemon
3 cups sugar	Granulated sugar
1 tablespoon orange-blossom water	

Wash eggplant. Remove stems. Boil until tender. Remove from fire. Place in cloth sack. Squeeze thoroughly until all water is removed. Remove from sack and spread out to dry.

Meanwhile, combine water, 3 cups sugar, orange-blossom water, clove, and lemon juice and boil until thick. When eggplants are dry, dip in syrup, then in granulated sugar.

FIG CONSERVE *Teen ma'qood*

3 pounds dry figs
2 cups sugar
1 cup water
Juice of 1 lemon
2 pounds chopped nuts
1 tablespoon anise seeds
3 pint jars

Wash and dry figs. Cut in quarters. Boil the sugar, water and lemon juice together. When syrupy, add figs. Cook on low fire until thick. Remove from fire and add chopped nuts and anise seeds. Cool and store in jars.

STUFFED FIGS *Teen mihshee*

1 pound dried whole figs
1 cup orange juice
1 tablespoon lemon juice
1 tablespoon grated lemon peel
3 tablespoons sugar
1 cup almonds (or pecans)
1/2 cup sugar

Remove stems from figs. Combine orange juice, lemon juice, peel and the 3 tablespoons sugar. Add figs and heat mixture to boiling point. Simmer in covered saucepan until fruit is tender. Drain well. Cool. Insert knife in stem end of fig and stuff each fig with an almond. Close opening and roll figs in 1/2 cup sugar. Dry overnight before storing.

MISKEE SWEETS *Hilwat miskee*

3 pounds granulated sugar
2 cups water
1 egg white
1 teaspoon lemon juice
2 tablespoons finely ground *miskee* (gum mastic)

Stir sugar, water, and egg white with a metal spoon in heavy saucepan. Place over high heat, stirring until mixture becomes syrupy. When it reaches rolling boil and rises in sauce-pan, spray with ice-cold water and remove from fire. Skim, place over heat again until syrup has thickened. (To test syrup, drop a little syrup in a small cup of ice water. When firm ball can be formed with fingers, syrup is ready). Remove from heat and cover with with clean cloth until slightly cooled. Then whip with heavy wooden pestle until smooth and creamy. Add *miskee* (ground with a little sugar to prevent sticking) and continue to whip until thick and very white. Refrigerate before serving.

CANDIED ORANGE, GRAPEFRUIT, OR LEMON PEEL *Qish'r bur-d-kan, trunj, ow limoon ma'qood*

Cut 1 pound rind into long narrow strips. Cover with water. Boil 30 minutes. Drain thoroughly. Cover again with cold water. Heat to boiling again and then drain. Repeat this procedure 3 times. Drain. Add 1-1/2 cups light corn syrup. Cook slowly until rind is translucent. Drain. Roll in granulated sugar.

WATERMELON PRESERVES *But-teekh mou-ra-ba*

  1 pound watermelon rind **1/2 lemon, sliced thin**
  1 tablespoon lime juice or salt **1/2 stick cinnamon**
  2 quarts water **3 pint jars**
  2 cups granulated sugar

Pare the rind and remove pink edge. Cut into 1-inch cubes and let stand overnight in solution of lime or salt and 1 quart water. Drain and rinse with cold water. Cover with boiling water and cook 15 minutes. Drain. Combine sugar with 1 quart water and boil 5 minutes. Add rind, lemon slices, and cinnamon. Cook rapidly until rind is clear. Let stand in syrup overnight. Reheat to boiling, pour into sterile jars, and seal. *Yield: 3 pints*.

ALMOND CANDY *Low-zee-yee*

  2 egg whites **2 teaspoons rose water**
  2 pounds blanched almonds, **Maraschino cherries**
   ground fine **Red and green food coloring**
  2 tablespoons cream **Granulated sugar**
  2 teaspoons almond extract
  1 pound confectioners' sugar

Beat egg whites until stiff. Gradually blend in almonds, cream, almond extract, sugar, and rose water until mixture is stiff enough to handle. Roll into small balls. Flatten each ball and place a cherry in center. Fold mixture around cherry. Roll one side of candy in red sugar, the other half in green sugar (granulated sugar with food coloring added.)

Mamool—recipe on page 104

Fillo Bird's Nests—recipe on page 101

Tray filled with baklawa logs and Sa-bi-et il sit finger pastries - Ricotta pastries - Accordion pleated pastries - date filled bracelets - nut-filled butter cookies)

PASTRIES AND DESSERTS

Hiloo

Syrians and Lebanese along with other Mediterranean countries like sweets of all descriptions. *Baklawa* with its many delicate layers of thin-pastry sheets heads the list of sweets fit for the Kings. Filled with pistachios or walnuts, sugar, orange-flower water and topped with more layers of pastry brushed with a clarified butter, it is prepared in many various shapes; in diamond shapes, in bird's nest shapes, *"sabi' et il-sit"* (lady's fingers) and made into logs.

There is a great deal of patience involved in making *baklawa* dough. Sis and I were always called in to help Mom stretch dough for the making of *baklawa* on our round oak dining room table covered with white tablecloth. This tedious and time-consuming task was well worth the flakiest and tastiest pastry dough for the making of dozens of trays of *baklawa*.

Starting from the center of the table, we began stretching the dough out to the edge of the table. The dough stretches easily and becomes tissue-thin. After the dough is stretched, it is left to stiffen at room temperature. When the sheets begin to feel like paper, they are cut into the desired lengths to fit the pans in which they will be baked. If there are any sheets left over, they can be frozen .

While visiting in San Diego, I learned how to make *Warbat il 'oshta* from the people who migrated there from **Ramallah** (near **Jerusalem**) and prepare it for many of my parties. It has become my most sought-after recipe. This flaky fillo dough is filled with ricotta cheese and drizzled with a simple syrup that has a hint of orange-flower water in it. I joined those same ladies of **Ramallah** at their church hall in San Diego in the making of *Knafee* (similar to a shredded wheat) - their hands working fast rubbing clarified butter into the dough to soften it. Some of the fillings used were pistachio nuts and others were filled with ricotta cheese. Others were made into *mabruma bil fistuq* (pistachio filled twist).

While all sorts of sweets are sold in the Middle East, the pastries are not prepared for every day meals. They are served during holiday seasons, weddings, baptisms, on other special occasions and to guests. Desserts usually consist of fresh fruits like figs, grapes, and melons, apricots and a multitude of other fruits that are so plentiful in the summer. During winter months, puddings like *almaseeyee, roz eb haleeb* and many preserves and candied fruits are served.

DIAMOND PASTRY DELIGHTS *Baklawa*

1 pound pastry sheets (Fillo dough) **9"x13" baking tray**
1-1/2 cups clarified butter

Combine the following ingredients:

4 cups ground English walnuts **1 teaspoon orange blossom water**
1/2 cup sugar **2 tablespoons clarified butter**

Brush baking tray with melted butter. Place pastry sheet on bottom of pan and brush with butter. Repeat until you have piled up 15 pastry sheets, each one brushed with butter. Distribute the nut mixture (about 1/2 inch thick) over bed of pastry sheets. Then add 15 more pastry sheets on top of mixture, brushing each sheet with butter. With sharp knife, cut into 1-1/2" diamond shape. Place pan on second rack of oven. Bake in preheated oven (325°) for 45 minutes until top turns a light golden shade. Prepare syrup earlier in the day so it will be cold when *baklawa* is baked. *Yield: 50 cuts.*

NOTE: It is important to use clarified butter (unsalted) butter for the delicate taste of this pastry.

Diamond Pastry Delights (Baklawa)

Baklawa rolls

SYRUP *Qatar lil baklawa* (Use this same syrup for all fillo dough recipes)

3 cups sugar
2 cups water
Juice of 1 lemon
1 teaspoon orange blossom water *mazaher*

Mix sugar and water until sugar is dissolved. Bring to a boil. Add lemon juice; cook 15 minutes on medium fire and then add orange blossom water. Pour the hot syrup slowly over the cold *baklawa*.

(NOTE: Never pour hot syrup over hot baklawa. One or the other should be cold. If making many trays of baklawa, it would be wise to double the syrup recipe and have it on hand for immediate use.)

THIS IS A **Fast** way to make Baklawa THAT PRODUCES AN EXCELLENT TRAY:

1 package fillo dough
1-1/2 pound clarified butter, melted
Same amount of filling as previous recipe

Preheat oven to 450°. Brush baking tray with butter. Place half of the fillo dough on the buttered tray. At this point <u>do not</u> place any butter on the fillo dough. Place filling over the 15 layers and top with the remaining 15 layers of fillo dough. Cut into diamond shapes. Pour clarified butter over all. Bake in 450° oven for 8 minutes. Turn oven off. Leave in oven for 45 minutes. (**Do not open oven during this time**). Remove from oven and pour cool syrup on warm baklawa.

BAKLAWA ROLLS   *Terrific logs for fast party desserts*

1 package fillo dough
1 pound clarified butter, melted
4 cups ground English walnuts
1/2 cup sugar
1 tablespoon butter
1/4 teaspoon orange blossom water

Fillo dough should be at room temperature. Mix together 1/2 cup sugar with 4 cups chopped nuts. Add 1 tablespoon melted butter and 1/4 teaspoon orange blossom water and mix well. Butter the baking tray. Preheat oven to 325°.

After opening package of fillo dough, carefully cover with plastic and damp cloth to prevent drying. (For best results, let the frozen fillo dough thaw in refrigerator overnight). Brush each sheet with butter until you have 4 sheets buttered. Place on top of one another. When 4th sheet is buttered, place one cup of the nut mixture across the wide bottom end of the dough and fold in edges; roll like a jelly roll. Place seam side down in baking tray and cut half-way through each cut in 1-1/2 inch pieces at a sharp angle (do not cut all the way through). Brush each roll with butter. Place tray on middle shelf of oven and bake for 30 minutes, then on top shelf of oven for another five minutes until a golden shade. Remove from oven and pour cold syrup over each roll. *Yield: 5 rolls (10 to 12 cuts per roll)*

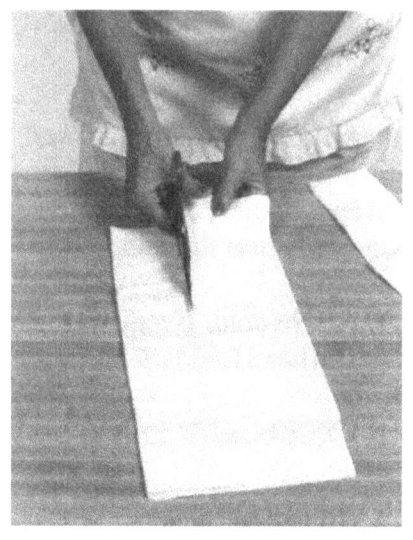

Helen demonstrates how to make Ricotta pastries at one of her cooking classes.

#1. Cutting fillo dough

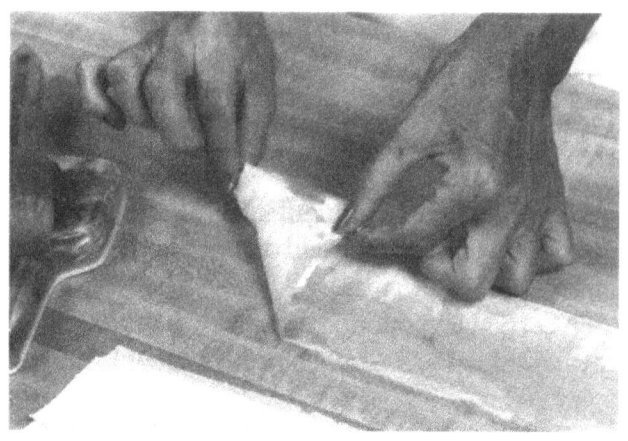

#4. Folding flag-style, brushing each fold with butter

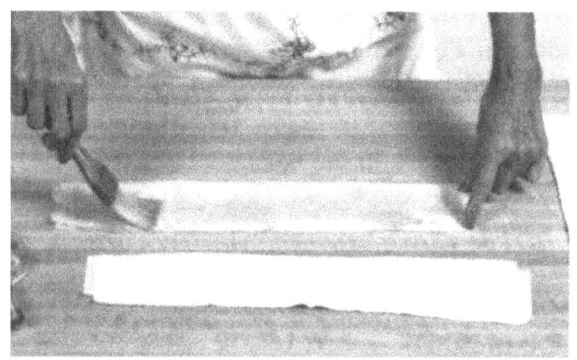

#2. Brushing layers with butter

#5. Brushing last fold with butter

RICOTTA PASTRIES *Warbat il 'oshta* or *Shybe-yat*

>1 pound clarfied butter
>1 15 oz. carton ricotta cheese
>1 egg
>1 tablespoon sugar, optional
>1 package fillo dough
>   (approximately 30 sheets to a
>   14"x18" package)
>2 baking trays, 12"x18"

#3. Placing ricotta on corner

In a bowl, beat egg with wire whisk. Add sugar and ricotta cheese and mix thoroughly with wooden spoon.

Melt butter. Preheat oven to 350°. Cut fillo pastry into 4 equal portions 3-1/4" lengthwise with kitchen scissors through entire package of dough. Take one stack of fillo and set to one side to be used immediately. Cover remaining dough with wax paper topped with damp cloth so that dough will not dry out.

Take 4 strips of fillo, brushing each one with butter and place on top of each other. (You now have a stack of 4 strips of dough ready to fill and fold into a triangle shape. Place 1 tablespoon ricotta cheese mixture on bottom right hand corner and fold into flag shape, forming a triangle, brushing each fold with butter. There are approximately 7 folds for this size of a triangle. Place seam-side down on an ungreased baking tray. Bake 1 pan at a time. Position tray on middle shelf of oven and bake in 350° oven for 15 minutes until golden shade on bottom. Leave tray on same middle shelf in oven and broil for 30 seconds until light golden shade on top. Watch carefully so they do not get too brown.

Remove from oven. Transfer to another tray as there will be excess butter in tray which you can re-use. While pastries are hot, drizzle cold syrup over the pastries. *Yield: 23 to 25.*

NOTE: These can be frozen prior to baking. When ready to use, remove from freezer and place directly into preheated 350° oven and bake 15 minutes.

For PARTY SIZE PASTRIES, cut into six strips across and proceed with directions. *Yield: 36 from each package of fillo.*

FILLO BIRD'S NESTS, Accordian pleated *(photo on page 95)*

2 pounds fillo dough
4 cups clarified butter

FILLING:

6 cups chopped English walnuts
   or pistachios
1/2 cup sugar

1 tablespoon melted clarified butter
1 tablespoon orange blossom water

Mix together all filling ingredients. Place 1 pastry sheet on work table and brush with clarified butter. Fold in three's lengthwise. Cut in 3 equal portions. Place 1 tablespoon filling mixture in center. Fold edges over center accordion fashion. Place on ungreased baking tray. Place on middle shelf of 350° preheated oven and bake for 20-25 minutes until tops are a light golden shade. Remove from baking tray when cool. Pour cold syrup over warm pastries.

NOTE: For a festive look, add green food coloring to english walnuts and sprinkle in center. These keep well in refrigerator and are nice and crispy.

NUT RINGS: *'Ish il bul-bul*

    1/2 pound pastry sheets   **1/2 teaspoon cinnamon**
    1 pound chopped walnuts   **1/2 teaspoon cloves**
    1/4 cup sugar   **1 pound clarified butter, melted**

Combine walnuts, sugar and spices. Brush one pastry sheet with melted butter and sprinkle lightly with nut mixture. Cut pastry sheet in quarters (about 6 inches in length). Roll like cigars. Arrange in baking pan tightly, cut side down. Repeat until pastry sheets are used. Brush each roll generously with melted butter. Bake in moderate 350° oven for 30 minutes. Dip in syrup. *Yield: about 40 nut rings.*

ALMOND ROLLS *Lefet Lowz*

    6 eggs, separate yolk from white   **2 ounces whiskey**
    2 cups sugar   **1 pound fillo pastry sheets**
    2 pounds blanched ground almonds **1-1/2 pounds clarified butter**

Beat egg yolks until light. Add sugar. Beat until creamy. In separate bowl, beat egg whites until stiff. Add almonds and egg whites alternately to egg-yolk mixture. Mix in whiskey.

Place pastry sheets on work surface. Cover with damp towel to prevent sheets from drying out and becoming flaky. Brush each sheet with butter until you have 3 sheets buttered. When third sheet is buttered, pour 1/4 of mixture across wide bottom end of pastry and roll like a jelly roll, turning ends in to retain mixture. Repeat until there are 5 almond rolls. Place side by side in pan, seam side down, and brush with melted butter. Bake 30 minutes in moderate 350° oven. Remove from oven. Pour cold syrup over hot pastry. Slice immediately. *Yield: 5 Almond Rolls.*

KNAFEE (also known as *Kataifi* - shredded dough)

If dough is frozen, let it thaw in refrigerator overnight. Before using, let set at room temperature for 2 hours.

    1 pound knafee dough   **2 cups simple syrup**
    2 pounds ricotta cheese   **Baking dish, 9"x13"**
    1 pound clarified butter

Place dough in a large bowl. Loosen by gently pulling strands of dough apart with both hands. Sprinkle with a little water to dampen dough, and keep covered with a damp cloth until ready to use. Pour melted butter over the shredded dough. Blend thoroughly with both hands by rubbing butter into the dough until it is saturated. Divide the mixture in half. Put half of the mixture on the bottom of a baking dish. Arrange cheese over the dough. Cover with remaining dough. Press down slightly. Cut in 2 inch squares.

Bake in preheated 300° over for 45 minutes to 1 hour. add cold *baklawa* syrup while *knafee* is hot. Keep some syrup on the side in a pitcher for those who want to drench their *knafee* to a heavenly sweetness.

NOTE: You can also use the baklawa nut filling in place of the ricotta filling. (This dessert can be made in advance of a party. Freeze unbaked and bake it the day of the party, from freezer to oven.)

STUFFED SHREDDED WHEAT (this is another form of *Knafee* made from boxed shredded wheat)

    1 box shredded wheat (9 to a box)   Clarified butter
    1 quart milk

Soak shredded wheat in cold milk until softened. Make center opening from end to end of each shredded wheat and fill, using same filling as that for *Ma'mool*. Brush baking pan with butter and place shredded wheat side by side in pan. Brush tops heavily with butter. Bake in slow 250° oven until golden brown, approximately 30 minutes. Remove from oven and cool. Pour *baklawa* syrup over all.

SESAME PASTRY DELIGHTS *Baklawa simsum*

    1/4 pound sesame seeds   1 teaspoon cinnamon
    3 tablespoons butter   1/2 teaspoon lemon rind
    1 pound blanched almonds, ground fine   1 pound clarified butter
    3/4 cup sugar   1 pound pastry sheets

Saute sesame seeds in 3 tablespoons butter until golden brown. Combine sesame, almonds, sugar, cinnamon, and lemon rind in a dish. Brush bottom of pan with melted butter and place one pastry sheet, brushed with melted butter, on bottom of pan. Repeat until you have 4 sheets on bottom of pan. Sprinkle with nut mixture, repeating until nut mixture has been consumed. Top with 4 buttered sheets of pastry. (See *Baklawa* recipe for cutting instructions.) Bake at 370° for 30 minutes, then reduce oven to 350° and bake an additional 25 minutes or until a golden shade. *Yield: 24 Sesame Pastry Delights*. Top with same syrup as in Baklawa.

BUTTER COOKIES *Gribee*

    1 cup clarified butter, chilled   1 tablespoon rose water
    1 cup super-fine sugar   2 cups flour

In food processor with steel blade, cream butter, adding sugar and rose water and process until fluffy. Add flour and pulsate (turning motor off and on) until flour disappears and mixture is soft. Place dough in bowl. Pinch off dough the size of golf balls and shape as desired. (Traditionally about 2-1/4" in circumference indented in center with your finger). Place on ungreased baking tray and bake in 300° oven for 15-20 minutes until bottoms are very light brown. Tops will remain white. Let cool several hours before removing from pan. *Yield: 25 cookies.*

If you don't have a Food Processor, try this recipe for making *GRIBEE*

3/4 cup clarified butter **1/4 teaspoon rose water**
1 cup granulated sugar **3 cups flour**

Cream the butter and add sugar and rose water, creaming with mixer until fluffy. Add flour and knead well. Shape as desired in doughnut shapes pressing center with finger or shape as a finger and place in dry baking pan. Bake in slow 300° oven about 15 minutes until bottoms are very light brown. Leave set in baking pan several hours to cool before removing from pan. *Yield: 32 cookies.*

GRIBEE PARTY RECIPE SERVING 60

2 cups clarified butter, chilled **4 cups flour (scant)**
2 cups powdered sugar

Cream butter until white. Add sugar and continue beating until fluffy. Add flour, kneading well. Form into 5 balls. Flour a pastry board lightly. Roll each ball like a long rope, 1-1/2" in circumference. Cut at a diagonal. Bake on top shelf of a preheated 250° oven about 15 minutes. Remove from oven and let cool 2 hours before removing from tray. *Yield: 60 cuts.*

NUT-FILLED CAKES *Ma'mool (photo on page 95)*

1-1/2 cups clarified butter **3 cups flour**
1/2 cup sugar **1 teaspoon orange flower water**
1/2 cup evaporated milk

Cream together butter and sugar until light. Add the milk and flour and knead well. (I use my food processor and get a perfect blend). Form dough into small round balls, 2 inches in circumference. Make an indentation and fill with 1 teaspoon nut mixture. Close the top, sealing dough together. Place in *ma'mool* mold to form pattern on bottom. With fingers, flatten top of dough. Tap mold on board or table to release *ma'mool*. Place on ungreased baking tray. (Pattern will be on top).

Preheat oven to 325°. Place tray on middle shelf of oven and bake 15 minutes. Then move tray to upper shelf of oven and bake another 5 minutes. Do not remove from tray until completely cool. Sprinkle with powdered sugar. *Yield: 28 cakes.*

FILLING: Combine following ingredients:

- 2 cups ground english walnuts
- 1/4 cup sugar
- 2 tablespoons clarified butter
- 1 teaspoon orange blossom water

NOTE: Ma'mool molds are available at stores listed in Shoppers' Guide.

MA'MOOL Party Serving for 144.

- 6 cups clarified butter, room temperature
- 2 cups sugar
- 12 cups flour
- 2 cups evaporated milk

Use same procedure as above. For the filling, use 8 cups of nuts and 1 cup sugar, 1/2 cup clarified butter, 2 tablespoons orange blossom water. *Yield: approximately 144.*

DATE CRESCENTS *Ujwee*

- 2 cups clarified butter
- 3/4 cup granulated sugar
- 3 eggs, beaten lightly
- 6 cups all-purpose flour
- 2 oz. whiskey
- 1 tablespoon crushed mahleb (optional)

Cream butter with sugar. Mix in the eggs, flour and whiskey and knead well. Set to one side for 2 hours.

FILLING:
- 2 pounds dates, chopped
- 1/4 cup clarified butter
- 1 cup english walnuts, chopped

Mix together the above ingredients. Shape into 1-1/2" rolls like the shape of a date. Roll out the dough and wrap around the date mixture, or encase the dates in a circle of dough, like a small bracelet. Place on ungreased baking tray and bake at 350° for 20 minutes until golden shade. When cool, sprinkle with powdered sugar. *Yield: 72.*

SESAME COOKIES *Barazek* (these declicious cookies go fast at your church bazaar)

- One pound sweet butter
- 1-3/4 cups sugar
- 6 cups all-purpose flour
- 2 teaspoons baking powder
- 1 cup cold milk
- 2 cups sesame seeds
- 1 cup light syrup
- 3 tablespoons cold water

Cream butter until fluffy. Add sugar and continue beating until well blended. Mix together the baking powder and flour. Add to the butter-sugar mixture and mix well. Add milk and knead all ingredients well. Divide dough into balls the size of grapefruit. Place each ball between 2 layers of wax paper. Roll to 1/8 inch thickness and cut in circles 3 inches in diameter.

Combine syrup and water. Spread each cookie with the syrup mixture and dip coated side into a bowl of sesame seeds covering top completely. Bake in 375º oven 12 minutes. Remove from tray when cool. *Yield: 76.*

RICE CUSTARD *Roz eb haleeb* (the kids love this custard - grown-ups too!)

1 quart milk
1/4 cup rice, medium grain, cooked
3 tablespoons cornstarch, sifted
1/2 cup sugar
1 teaspoon rose water

Heat milk on medium fire until crust forms, about 15 minutes. Add precooked rice. Stir slowly until milk boils. Cook on low fire for 30 minutes. Mix cornstarch with 6 tablespoons water to dissolve cornstarch. Add to milk-rice mixture; stir ten minutes and add sugar, stirring until custard begins to get thick. Add rose water, stir for 1 minute and remove from fire. Cool and pour into custard cups. Garnish with crushed pistachios. *Serves 6.*

Micro-tip: Heat milk in the microwave on high for 15 minutes. Add precooked rice. Micro on power level 8 for 10 minutes. In a small bowl, mix cornstarch with water. Add to milk-rice mixture along with sugar. Cook in micro on power level 8 for 5 minutes. Remove, stir and cook an additional 10 minutes. Stir in the rose water and cook 1 minute.

VANILLA PUDDING *Almaseeyee*

1 quart milk
3/4 cup sugar
3 tablespoons cornstarch
1 teaspoon orange-blossom water
Blanched almonds

Bring milk to a boil on low fire until crust forms on top. Add sugar and stir until boiling. Dissolve cornstarch thoroughly with 3 tablespoons water. Add to milk. Cook on low fire and stir constantly until pudding begins to thicken. Add orange-blossom water and cook 1 minute longer, stirring well. Pour into custard cups and garnish with almonds. *Serves 4.* (Mixture will thicken when it cools).

Qamheeyee *Whole wheat kernels*

2 cups whole wheat kernels
1/4 teaspoon salt
Bowl of sugar
Bowl of English walnuts
Bowl of white raisins

Rinse wheat. Place in 2 quart saucepan. Add 1/4 teaspoon salt, cover with water at least one inch above kernels. Bring to a rolling boil, cover pot, reduce heat to medium and cook until tender. If necessary add additional water while cooking. *Serve in dessert dishes. Pass the sugar, walnuts and raisins around for guests to add to the Qamheeyee.* **(In Syria and Lebanon, this is served to guests celebrating a baby's first tooth)**

MILK FARINA *Laqmet il hilwee*

2 quarts milk
2 cups farina
1/2 cup clarified butter

Mix farina with the milk. Place on medium fire. Stir until it comes to a boil and cook for 5 minutes. Melt butter and use half the amount on bottom of tray. Pour the cooked farina on top. Flatten it out and smooth with your hand; pour the remainder of the butter on top. Cool, cut into squares, and bake to a light brown in moderate 350° oven. Serve warm. Pour cold simple syrup over all. *Serves 8.*

HALAWA CAKE

1 cup clarified butter
1/2 cup powdered sugar
5 eggs, separated
2 cups farina
1 teaspoon cinnamon
1 teaspoon baking powder
1 teaspoon vanilla
1 cup chopped blanched almonds
12"x15" baking pan

Cream butter, add sugar. Beat egg whites stiff. Alternately, add egg whites, beaten yolks, farina, and cinnamon to butter-sugar mixture. Add baking powder, vanilla and almonds. Pour in greased baking pan and bake in moderate 350° oven for 30 minutes.

SYRUP: Boil 3 cups sugar and 2 cups water for 30 minutes. Pour over cake as soon as it is removed from oven. *Serves 10.*

HALAWA DIAMONDS

1 quart milk
1-1/2 cup sugar
1/4 pound clarified butter
1 cup farina
Cinnamon
Walnut halves

Boil milk, add sugar, and cook 10 minutes. Heat butter in heavy saucepan. Add farina to butter and stir constantly until farina is golden brown. Add milk slowly, stirring until mixture thickens. Pour mixture into 9-inch square greased pan and sprinkle with cinnamon. Cool for 1 hour. Cut in diamond-shaped pieces, placing a walnut half in the center of each. *Serves 10.*

SESAME CANDY *Sikkar simsum* (The Kymeeyee families in Canton, Ohio were known to make the best candies and a special treat is this sesame candy that the Albert family always served)

2 cups sesame seeds
1/2 cup honey   (Ex. 3; 17)
1/2 cup light brown sugar
1/2 teaspoon ground cinnamon
1/4 teaspoon ground ginger (optional)

Have on hand: a teflon skillet, a bowl for sesame seeds, bowl for mixing syrup, a 7-1/2" x 11-1/2" baking tray, and a bowl with ice water to dip metal spatula.

Brush baking tray with oil. Set aside. In a teflon skillet stir sesame seeds constantly over medium high heat until seeds are a golden shade, about 7 minutes. Remove all seeds from skillet and place in a bowl. Set to one side.

Mix together honey, brown sugar, cinnamon and ginger. Place in skillet and slowly bring to a boil over medium heat, stirring until mixture comes to a rolling boil, then cook for 2 more minutes. Remove and pour immediately into the sesame seeds, mixing with a metal stirring spoon. Quickly spoon out the hot sesame seed mixture into the oiled tray, using a metal spatula dipped into cold water to press mixture smoothly onto the entire tray.

Cool about 15 minutes and while still lukewarm, loosen the candy with spatula around the edge. The slab of candy will lift out easily as you place it on a cutting surface. Cut into squares with a sharp knife.

These will go fast. If there any left, when cool, store them in an airtight container.

Following are Greek recipes I've collected down through the years from friend Irene Doney.

SESAME TWIST COOKIES *Koulourakia*

1-1/2 pounds butter, room temperature
1 cup oil
2-1/2 cups sugar, super-fine
1 shot whiskey
1 teaspoon vanilla
6 eggs
½ cup cold milk
12-13 cups flour
6 teaspoon baking powder
2 eggs beaten with 1 tablespoon water
Sesame seeds

Cream butter and gradually add in sugar. Then eggs, one by one. Add whiskey, vanilla, milk. Mix in flour and baking powder last. Roll about 2-1/2 inches long and thick like a cigar. (If you need to add flour to keep the dough from sticking to your hands, add another cup.) Then form into a twist.

DIPPING BATTER: Mix 2 eggs with 2 teaspoons water. Dip one side of twist in egg batter, then in sesame seeds. Place in baking tray and bake in 375° oven for 20 minutes until golden brown.

The following is one of my all-time favorites:

GALATOBOUREKO

12"x 16" baking pan
1 quart milk
1 cup farina
1 teaspoon salt
6 eggs

1 pound fillo dough
¾ cup sugar
6 tablespoon clarified butter
1 teaspoon vanilla
Syrup

Prepare syrup and set aside to cool.

Heat milk. Slowly add farina, stirring constantly. Add salt and boil until thick, about 5 minutes. In another bowl, beat eggs until light, and gradually beat in ¾ cup sugar. Fold into the farina mixture. Continue to cook, stirring constantly for about 3 minutes. Remove from heat and add butter. Stir until incorporated. Add vanilla. Stir occasionally. Brush baking pan with butter. Place ½ package of fillo dough on baking pan, brushing each sheet with butter. Spread farina mixture over pastry. Cover with remaining pastry, brushing each sheet with butter. Cut through top of pastry in 2 inch squares. Bake in preheated 350° oven for 45 minutes until golden. Remove from oven. When lukewarm, cut through custard layer to bottom. Pour cool syrup over the warm Galatoboureko.

SYRUP: Mix together 3 cups sugar, 2 cups water, 1 teaspoon lemon juice. Bring to a boil, and simmer for 15 minutes. When cool pour over the warm Galataboureko..

FISH

Samek

(Matt. 4:18-21; Mark 1:16, 19; Numbers 11:5)

The waters of the Mediterranean offer a wealth of sea food, including red snapper, crayfish, lobsters, shrimp, crab, scallops, clams, oysters, mussels, and anchovies. The sardine is abundant; a favorite is *barboor* (red mullet) along with Sultan Ibrahim's Red Snapper.

In some restaurants the patron may choose the fish and often watch it being cooked. *Taratoor* (a sauce of *tahini* [sesame oil], lemon juice, and garlic) is usually served with the fish course.

BAKED STUFFED RED SNAPPER *Sultan Ibrahim* — Hamoor, a smaller red snapper found only in the Meditteranean.

```
1 large red snapper, 4-1/2 pounds dressed (keep head and tail on)
    (have your fish market remove the eyes and bones)
Salad oil                           Butter
1/2 cup pine nuts or almonds        1/2 cup rice
1 small onion, chopped              1 tablespoon chopped parsley
                                    Salt and pepper to taste
```

Spread fish open. Wash thoroughly and wipe dry. Sprinkle inside and out with salt. Let fish stand for 10 minutes; drain. Brush roasting pan with oil. Place fish in pan and brush oil on top of fish.

Brown pine nuts and onion in a small amount of butter. Pre-cook the rice in 1 cup of boiling water for 20 minutes. Add rest of ingredients. Lightly fill cavity with rice dressing. Hold together with toothpicks. Bake fish in hot 400° oven for 10 minutes, then reduce heat to 350°. Brush fish with oil every 10 minutes. Continue baking approximately 40 minutes. Garnish with pomegranate seeds and lemon slices. Serves 8. *(This is a nice Lenten meal accompanied with fried green tomato slices, fried eggplant slices and fried potatoes)*

BAKED STUFFED FISH *Samek mihshee*

```
2 pound bass                        1 small onion, chopped
1 small bass                        1/2 cup rice
Oil                                 1 tablespoon chopped parsley
1/2 cup pine nuts or almonds        Salt and pepper to taste
```

Remove backbone and small bones of larger bass. Spread fish open. Wash thoroughly and wipe dry. Rub inside and out with salt. Let fish stand for 10 minutes; drain.

Cut small bass in half. Fry in hot oil. Remove meat from bones. Brown pine nuts and onion in a small amount of oil. Cook the rice in 1 cup boiling water. Add to rest of ingredients with parsley, salt and pepper. Stuff bass and hold together with toothpicks. Brush skin thoroughly with salad oil. Brush pan with oil and bake fish in very hot 500° oven for 10 minutes, then reduce heat to 400°. Continue baking until golden brown, approximately 30 to 35 minutes. Serve with *Taratoor* dressing. Garnish with parsley and lemon slices. *Serves 4.*

BAKED HALIBUT *Tajin* (an elegant dish)

> 1 3 pound Halibut
> 1 pound pine nuts
> 1 onion, chopped fine
> 6 tablespoons Taratoor (Sesame sauce)
> Chopped parsley
> Pomegranate seeds (optional)

Preheat oven to 350°. Wash halibut thoroughly in cool water. Brush baking tray with oil. Place halibut on tray and bake until fish appears to be tender and flaky (approximately 15 to 20 minutes on each side). Remove from oven. Fish is now flaky enough to remove bones. Place on platter and put to one side to cool. Brown chopped onion in oil. Strain and discard onion. Reserve oil that onion was cooked in and use to brown pine nuts. Remove pine nuts from oil and set aside. Take whatever oil remains in skillet and sprinkle over fish. Spoon *taratoor* dressing over entire cooked fish until completely covered. Garnish with parsley, pine nuts, and pomegranate seeds. Serve with Rice and Spinach with lemon. *Serves 4.*

GRILLED TROUT *Samek mishwee* (A real treat served off the grill)

> **8 trout fillets (4 ounces each)**

Combine the following:
> 3 tablespoons lemon juice
> 1 tablespoon Dijon mustard
> 3 cloves garlic, minced
> 1/8 teaspoon each salt and pepper

Gradually stir in 2 tablespoons olive oil. Marinade the trout in refrigerator for half an hour. Oil the grill and place trout fillets, flesh side down. Cook 2 minutes over hot coals. Gently turn trout with 2 spatulas and cook another 2 minutes until done (flakes esily with a fork). Boil left-over marinade for 1 minute and serve with trout. Garnish with chopped chives. *Serves 6.*

BAKED FISH *Samek makhbooz*

Clean one large bass or blue pike thoroughly. Salt both sides and set overnight in refrigerator. Following day drain. Brush skin thoroughly with oil on both sides. Place in baking pan and bake in very hot 450° oven for 30 minutes. Serve with *Taratoor* dressing and lemon slices. *Serves 2.*

COD WITH SAUCE *Samek al qud ma' marqet*

2 pounds cod	1 clove garlic, crushed
Oil	1 tablespoon chopped parsley
3 ripe tomatoes, quartered	
1/8 teaspoon each of salt and pepper	

Flour pieces of cod which have been well soaked in salt water. Brown them in very hot oil in skillet. Remove cod and keep hot. Place peeled tomatoes in skillet. Add seasonings and garlic. The tomatoes will form a sauce which is then poured over the cod. Garnish with chopped parsley. *Serves 4.*

FLOUNDER WITH MUSHROOM SAUCE *Samek ma' fotir*

3 pounds flounder fillets	1 sprig each of sweet basil and thyme
1/2 cup water	1/2 teaspoon allspice
1 tablespoon butter	2 sprigs parsley
2 tablespoons flour	1 bay leaf
1/2 cup canned mushrooms, chopped	Salt and pepper to taste

Rub fish with salt and pepper. Bake with 1/2 cup water at 375° for 25 minutes. Remove from oven. Melt butter, add flour, and stir until smooth. Remove from heat and add remaining ingredients and liquid from fish. Cook over low heat, stirring constantly until thickened. Score top of fish, pour sauce over fish, and bake in oven 15 minutes longer. *Serves 6.*

HOT RED MULLETS *Samek barboor*

8 mullets	Anchovy fillets
Oil	12 black olives
1 clove garlic	Chopped parsley
1 cup tomatoes	Lemon wedges

Flour the fish and fry them in very hot oil. While the fish are frying, in another pan saute garlic in oil. Add peeled tomatoes to garlic and simmer a few minutes. Remove from fire, add anchovy fillets and olives. Arrange fish on an oval dish. Cover with sauce, sprinkle parsley over sauce, and place lemon wedges around edge of platter. *Serves 4.* NOTE: Take pieces of Syrian thin bread *marquq* and fry in the hot oil. Place a platter of this crispy bread along side the fish. This also removes the fish taste from the oil and you can re-use the oil.

FISH KIBBY *Kibbet samek*

1-1/2 pounds raw shrimp, peeled, and deveined
1 pound white fish (cod or flounder)
2 cups wheat, fine grain

Peel of 1 orange
1 medium size onion, grated
1 tablespoon fresh coriander,
1 large baking tray (10" x 17")

INGREDIENTS FOR FILLING:
3 large onions
1/2 cup pine nuts

1 cup olive oil

Soak wheat 10 minutes. Drain off water and refrigerate until grains are soft, about 2 hours. Grind shrimp and fish. Add to the wheat. Add rest of ingredients and knead well. Julienne 3 large onions and saute them in 3 tablespoons olive oil. Remove onions and saute the pine nuts. Oil baking tray. Place onions on bottom of oiled tray and pine nuts on top of the onions. Take patties of *kibby samek* and place on top of onion-nut mixture. Dip your hand in cold water and keep entire top smooth. Score diagonally and pour 1 cup oil over the entire top. Bake in preheated 425° oven for 30 minutes. Place under broiler until the top is a golden brown shade. (*This **Tripoli** recipe comes from Laurice Neam, Washington, D.C.. Her husband Jack's family comes from Tripoli where there is an abundance of sea food*)

SAMKE HARRA **Fish with Hot Chili Sauce** (*I was treated to this fabulous entree at a party hosted in my honor by Mr. & Mrs. Malouf, attache to the Lebanese Embassy, prepared by Mr. Malouf's sister Sonia Malouf of Lebanon*)

1 4 pound grouper
5 medium ripe tomatoes, chopped
6 bunches fresh coriander leaves, chopped
10 cloves garlic, sliced
1 cup olive oil for frying

1/4 pound almonds, blanched
1/4 pound pine nuts
1/2 teaspoon each, salt, pepper
1/2 teaspoon hot chili pepper
2 teaspoons hot chili sauce

Clean and scale the fish. With paper towels, wipe dry. Sprinkle with salt. Cover and refrigerate for 1 hour. Bake fish in a 350° moderate oven for 35 minutes. When cool, take out the bones. Set head and tail to one side.

Heat the oil, saute the garlic until light brown. Add tomatoes, cover and simmer for 15 minutes until tomatoes are thick. Add coriander, stir, cook on low fire. Add salt and peppers and hot sauce, cooking a few more minutes.

Pour 2 tablespoons of the oil in another frying pan. Saute the almonds until light brown, then add pine nuts until a golden shade. When fish is baked, remove skin and bones and discard. Place flesh in serving plate in a fish form. Put back the head and tail. Cover fish completely with sauce and garnish with almonds and pine nuts. Serve at room temperature. *Serves 6.*

SAYADEEYA *Fisherman's Stew* *(Father George Rados of Washington, D.C. keeps a freezer stocked with an ample supply of fish he catches from Chesapeake Bay. He shared this favorite recipe of his)*

2 pounds of haddock or halibut
Juice of 1 lemon
2 medium onions, chopped
1/2 cup olive oil
6 cups water
1 teaspoon cinnamon
Salt and pepper to taste
2 cups rice
1/2 cup pine nuts, toasted
1 teaspoon cumin powder

Wash fish. Cut into medium pieces. Salt and sprinkle lemon juice on fish. Set to one side for 30 minutes. Brown onions in oil until very dark brown. Remove from oil. Reserve the oil. Place onions in a pan of water and boil for 10 minutes. Add fish, cumin, cinnamon, salt and pepper. Cook until fish is cooked, about 10 minutes. Take 4 cups of the broth and reserved oil and cook the rice about 25 minutes. Place rice in a platter and layer fish on top. Sprinkle pine nuts over all. *Serves 6 to 8. Garnish with lemon wedges and parsley.*

TROUT, PAN FRIED *Samek miqlee*

4 trout, about 7" long
1 teaspoon salt
1/2 teaspoon pepper
1/2 cup flour
1/3 cup milk
1/2 cup olive oil
1/4 cup parsley, chopped

Combine flour, salt and pepper. Dip trout in milk; dredge in flour, coating completely. In a heavy skillet, saute trout in oil for 4 minutes on one side until browned. Turn and brown the other side for 4 minutes. *Serves 4. Serve with rice mixed with peas, a salad and hot talamee.*

LENTEN FOODS

Akal Syam

In Orthodox Catholic communities Lent marks the beginning of fasting and the cessation of games and dancing. In the villages the women exchange their bright colorful dresses for the somber and dark shades. The period of the Lenten fast is preceded by the *Marfeh* (Meat-fare and Cheese-fare weeks).

When the calendar shows the approach of the Easter season, women prepare for the Lenten fast. While some countries serve pancakes and rich soups and sausages prior to the Great Lent, **Syrians and Lebanese** serve many meat dishes along with stuffed cabbage and grape leaves and *Kibby*. Cheese-fare week brings to the table all kinds of cheeses. Just as the Great Lent ends with the breaking of the Easter egg, the boiled egg is the last food eaten prior to the Lenten fasting period.

Lenten dishes are prepared without meat but with vegetables and oil; oil gives foods an entirely different flavor from those cooked in any other way. Aside from the nutritional qualities, oil is also a preservative, making it possible to keep foods fresh for many days without spoiling. This is important because many Lenten foods are eaten cold.

Orthodox Christians abstain not only from meat and from poultry but derivatives thereof, i.e. eggs, milk, and cheese during all fasting days. Fasting is observed during the Great Lent, every Wednesday and Friday throughout the year (unless a feast takes place over the fast), and on all the fast days listed on the pages immediately following.

FASTS PRESCRIBED BY THE HOLY EASTERN ORTHODOX CHURCH   *IL SYAM*

The *Great Fast*. Beginning seven weeks before Easter, Lent is the most important period of the year for the Holy Eastern Orthodox Catholic Church. The fast is divided into two parts.

The first forty days commemorate the fast of Christ in the dessert. During this fast, according to the Scriptures, Satan appeared before Christ to tempt Him. **(Matt: 4:1-11)**

The Passion-week fast, a separate fast, commemorates the suffering and passion of Christ. Orthodox Christians abstain from meat and dairy foods, but children and sick persons need not.

A period of self-denial, contemplation, and prayer, the Great Fast begins on the Monday after Cheese-fare Sunday - forty days before Palm Sunday - and ends on the eve of Palm Sunday.

Holy Week, from the evening of Palm Sunday to Holy Saturday, is a special fast in honor of Christ's passion.

The *Weekly Fasts*. Each Wednesday and Friday is observed with fasting, unless a feast takes precedence over the fast. The fast on Wednesday is in memory of the betrayal of Christ; the fast on Friday is in memory of His Passion and death on the Cross.

The Fast of the Holy Apostles. Beginning on the Monday after All Saints' Sunday - the Sunday following Pentecost - and lasting until the Feast of the Holy Apostles (Peter and Paul) on June 29, this fast varies in length depending on the date of Easter.

The Fast of the Theotokos. Preceding the Feast of the Falling Asleep of the All-Holy Theotokos, this fast begins on August 1 and lasts until the day of the feast, August 15.

The Fast Before Christmas. Beginning on November 15, this fast lasts only until the day of the Feast of the Nativity, December 25.

Special Fast Days.

> August 29. The Beheading of St. John the Baptist.
> September 14. The Elevation of the Holy Cross.
> January 5. The Eve of the Epiphany.

When Fasting is forbidden.

The church forbids fasting during the following periods:

> From December 25 to January 5.
> The week after the Sunday of the Pharisee and the Publican.
> The week after Meat-fare Sunday requires abstinance only from flesh-meat.
> The week after Easter.
> The week after Pentecost.
> All Saturdays except Holy Saturday.

LENTEN PIES

Fatayer Syamee

LENTEN PIE DOUGH *'Ahjeen il fatayer syamee*

2 pounds flour
1/4 cup oil
1 package dry yeast
1 tablespoon salt
About 3 cups warm water
1/2 teaspoon *mahleb* (optional)

Mix ingredients and knead with water. Cover and let rest in warm place about 1-1/2 hours. When dough rises, cut into small sections 3 inches in diameter. Cover with cloth and allow to rise again for 30 minutes. Then flatten with your hand to almost as thin as pie dough. Use various fillings on following pages and either shape in triangles or leave face of pie open as suggested in recipes. *Yield: enough dough for 3 dozen pies.*

Placing chick-peas on dough before baking Fatayer homos (Chick-Pea Pie)

CHICK-PEA PIE *Fatayer homos*

Lenten Pie Dough
1 pound chick-peas

Soak chick-peas overnight with 1 teaspoon baking soda in water to cover. Wash thoroughly following day and drain off water until peas are dry. Place on pieces of dough (open-face pies). Bake in moderate 350° for 15 minutes, then place under broiler for a minute or two. Serve hot or cold. *Yield: 3 dozen pies.*

VEGETARIAN PIES *Ajeen ma' khuthra (Can't keep enough of these on hand)*

Basic pie dough, page 117
1 broiled eggplant
2 green squash
1 sweet red pepper, seeded
1 green pepper, seeded
3 tablespoons olive oil
1 large onion, chopped
6 sprigs parsley
1 tablespoon oregano
1/2 pound button mushrooms
2 teaspoons garlic powder
1 16 oz. can crushed tomatoes

Broil eggplant and peel. Slice the pulp. Wash the squash. Leave peel on. Cut in thin slices. Charbroil peppers and remove skins. Slice thin. Saute squash, peppers and onion in skillet with hot oil. Place in a bowl and mix together all of the ingredients except tomatoes. On a lightly floured board, shape dough into 3 inch rounds or 2 large rounds. Brush dough with olive oil Spoon tomatoes on top of dough and then arrange vegetables on top. Bake in 400º oven for 15 minutes until bottom is lightly browned. *Top with mozzarella cheese if you like. Yield: 2 large rounds. (For Christmas, add cooked spinach and form a tree in center of large pie, sprinkle on pomegranate seeds for a pretty picture and edge the pie with green and red peppers to look like a wreath - see photo on page XX)*

SPINACH PIE *Fatayer sabanigh*

Lenten Pie Dough, page 117
2 pounds frozen spinach, chopped, defrosted
1 teaspoons salt
3 onions, chopped fine
Juice of 3 lemons
1 cup ground English walnuts
1 teaspoon pepper
1/4 cup olive oil
1/2 teaspoon nutmeg

Squeeze moisture from spinach thoroughly In large bowl mix together all ingredients. Place spinach mixture on pieces of dough 3 inches in diameter and close into triangular shape. Brush oil on baking tray and arrange pies in rows. Bake in 350º oven for 15 minutes until bottoms are lightly browned. Place under broiler until tops of pies are lightly browned. Serve hot or cold. *Yield: 3 dozen pies. (These are great to take on a trip)*

THYME-SUMAC PIE *Fatayer za'tar - Mana-eesh (Travelers go out of their way to find a Middle-Eastern bakery that serves this mouth-watering fatayer hot out of the oven.)*

Lenten pie dough
4 tablespoons *za'tar*
Olive oil

Mix *za'tar* with enough olive oil to make a liquid paste for spreading on pieces of dough, 3 inches in diameter (open-face pies). Bake in 350º oven for 15 minutes, then place under broiler for 1/2 minute. Serve hot or cold. *Yield: 3 dozen pies.*

LENTEN KIBBY and FALAFEL

Kibby Syamee wa Falafel

FRIED POTATO KIBBY Qras Syamee miqlee

    2 pounds potatoes
    1 cup cracked wheat, fine
        (soak in cool tap water 10 minutes)
    Salt and pepper to taste
    1 cup flour

Boil potatoes. Peel and mash. Squeeze cracked wheat between palms to drain off the water. Knead potatoes and wheat together thoroughly. Add salt and pepper. Then blend in flour. Shape into small football-shaped *kibby*. Perforate one end and fill, using 1 teaspoon filling in each *kibby*.

FILLING;

    1 onion, sliced
    Olive oil
    1 cup pine nuts
    2 tablespoons lemon juice
    1/2 cup chick peas, dry (soaked overnight and cooked following day) (optional)

Saute onion in olive oil. Brown pine nuts in oil and mix with onion. Mix in the chick peas and lemon juice. Stuff *kibby*. Fry in corn or vegetable oil until golden brown. *Serves 6.*

POTATO KIBBY *Kibbet batata syamee*

    2 pounds potatoes
    1 cup cracked wheat, fine grain
    1 cup English walnuts, ground fine
    1 onion, grated
    Salt and pepper to taste
    1 large onion, sliced

Boil potatoes. Peel and mash. Rinse and soak cracked wheat a few minutes to soften. Squeeze wheat between palms to drain off the water. Mix all ingredients together. Add a little water and knead well. Place in platter and garnish with onion that has been sauteed in olive oil. *Serves 6.*

PUMPKIN KIBBY *Kibbet luqteen*

2 cups cracked wheat, #1	1 teaspoon salt
2 cups canned pumpkin	3/4 teaspoon cinnamon
1 cup flour	1/4 teaspoon nutmeg
1 medium onion, grated	3/4 teaspoon pepper

Rinse wheat. Drain water from wheat by cupping hands and squeezing out all moisture. Add all ingredients and blend together.

FILLING: Mix together 1 cup chick peas, canned; 1/2 cup sauteed pine nuts, 1 onion sauteed in oil, 1/2 teaspoon each salt, pepper, and cinnamon.

Oil a 9" x 13" baking pan. Spread half of kibby over bottom of pan. Spread filling evenly over layer and cover with remaining kibby. Score in diamond shapes or squares. Pour 1/4 cup oil over all. Bake in 350º oven for approximately 30 minutes. *Serves 8-10.* **Note: If mixture does not bind well, add more flour. If making into sphere shapes, chill in refrigerator for 2 hours before frying. Another filling: 1 cup chopped spinach, 1 small onion, 1/2 cup chick peas, 3 tablespoons lemon juice, 2 tablespoons olive oil, nutmeg, cinnamon, salt and pepper. Fry in hot oil or bake until golden brown.**

FALAFEL Recipe for this tasty vegetable burger comes from **Palestinian** friends Abla and Alex Khoury and featured daily at their "Kory's restaurant" in Indianapolis.

1 cup dried garbanzo beans	1/2 teaspoon baking soda
1 small onion, grated	2 teaspoons cumin powder
1/2 cup parsley leaves	3 teaspoons falafel spice
4 cloves garlic, crushed with salt	Corn or vegetable oil for frying

Soak beans in water overnight. Drain the following day. Place beans in food processor. Add onion, parsley, garlic, baking soda, cumin and falafel spices. Process until smooth. Let rest for 15 minutes, then refrigerate until chilled.

Pour oil 1 inch deep in a large skillet. Make sure that the oil is sizzling hot. Take a melon ball scoop and scoop up chick-pea mixture about 3/4" in diameter. Fry in hot oil until brown on all sides. They are cooked when they float to the top of the oil. If you do not have a scoop, moisten your hands with water and shape into small balls into 3/4" of diameter shape or unto 2" patties. *Yield: 24 balls or 12 patties.*

Serve in pocket bread and top with *Taratoor* dressing over a combination salad.

LENTIL DISHES

Akal'Addis (Gen. 25:34)

STRAINED LENTILS *Addis imsafa*

1/2 pound lentils	1/2 cup rice
6 cups water	1 onion, chopped

Sort and rinse lentils. Cook in water for 20 minutes. When cooked, reserve broth. Place lentils in colander and mash. Place mashed lentils in pan with broth. Add rice. Cook on low fire for 10 minutes, until all liquid is absorbed. Brown onion in olive oil. Garnish lentil platter with onions. *Serves 3.*

LENTILS AND WHEAT *Imjadara*

2 cups lentils	Salt and pepper to taste
8 cups water	2 onions, julienned
1 cup cracked wheat, coarse grind	1/2 cup olive oil

Sort lentils and rinse with cold water. Add lentils to pan filled with approximately 8 cups water. Do not cover. Boil about 20 minutes, until lentils are soft, then add wheat. Add salt and pepper and cook another 15 minutes, stirring occasionally to prevent sticking, until all liquid is absorbed. Fry onions in oil to a golden brown. Add oil to pan of lentils and garnish platter of lentils with fried onions. *Serves 4-6. A complete meal accompanied with yogurt and salata.* For leftovers, fix Lentils-Wheat with Kishik (*Imjadara marqoo'a*)

LENTIL-POTATO SOUP *'Addis imqala*
(a nutritious winter soup.....serve on any Lenten Friday)

2 cups lentils	2 large potatoes
6 cups water	1 large onion, chopped
Salt and pepper to taste	Olive oil
6 small onions	Lemon slices

Sort and rinse lentils. Cook in water for 15 minutes. Add salt and pepper. Quarter onions and add to cooked lentils. Cut potatoes in cubes and add to mixtue. Cook 10 more minutes. Brown chopped onion in olive oil and use with lemon slices to garnish. *Serves 4.*

LENTILS AND RICE *Imjadara ma' roz*

1 cup lentils	Salt and pepper to taste
6 cups water	2 large onions, julienned
1 cup rice	4 tablespoons olive oil

Sort lentils and rinse with cold water. Cook lentils in water over medium fire for 20 minutes. Add rice, salt and pepper and cook another 15 minutes. Fry onions in olive oil. Remove onions; pour oil over rice-lentil mixture and mix. Set until cool. Garnish with onions. *Serves 5.*

NOODLES AND LENTILS *Rishta*

1 cup lentils	2 cups flour
8 cups water	2 cups warm water
Salt and pepper	

Sort and rinse lentils. Cook in water for 20 minutes until tender. While lentils are cooking, prepare noodle dough. Mix flour with warm water and 1/2 teaspoon salt. Knead well. Place on floured board and roll with rolling pin. Cut in half. Sprinkle each half with flour. Roll each half as you would a jelly roll and cut in strips 1/2-inch wide. Add to cooked lentils and cook until done, about 30 minutes. Add salt and pepper to taste. *Serves 4.* (I've cooked this and at other times *Imjadara* many times on a snowy day when I couldn't get out to the grocery store.) Keep elbow macaroni on hand for a substitute, but there is nothing as tasty as making your own dough.... (make a small batch of Talamee to go with the meal and eat to your heart's content).

LENTILS WITH TOMATOES *'Addis ma' banadoora*

1 cup lentils	3 pimentos, chopped
2 cups water (add more if needed)	4 tablespoons olive oil
1 onion, chopped	2 cups tomatoes
1 green pepper, sliced	Salt and pepper to taste

Rinse lentils with cold water. Cook in boiling salted water 20 minutes. Saute onion, green pepper and pimentos in oil. Add tomatoes, salt, pepper and lentils and cook about 30 minutes, uncovered. Serve hot. *Serves 3-4.*

WHEAT AND VEGETABLE DISHES

Akal Qum-eh wa Khuthra

GREEN BEAN STEW *Yukhnee lubee akhthar*

    1 onion, diced
    1 clove garlic, chopped
    1/4 cup olive oil
    1 pound green beans
    1 cup water
    1 10-ounce can tomatoes (or tomato sauce)
    Salt and pepper to taste

Saute onion and garlic in oil. Cut beans in half. Add to onion and garlic. Cover and let steam 30 minutes, mixing frequently. Add water and tomatoes until even with beans. Add seasoning to taste. Cook 15 minutes or until tender. *Serves 4.* (For a tasty variation, omit tomatoes. Add 1 tablespoon crushed thyme, and 1 tablespoon lemon juice.)

LENTEN CABBAGE ROLLS *Yubraq Syamee*

    1 large head cabbage
    1 teaspoon salt
    2 cloves garlic, chopped
    Juice of 3 lemons

Carve out thick core from center of cabbage. Drop cabbage into salted boiling water, cored end down. Boil until leaves are softened. While boiling, loosen each leaf with a long fork, remove, and place in a dish to cool. Remove heavy center stems from the leaves. If leaves are large, cut in half. Fill each leaf with 1 teaspoon stuffing and roll in shape of a cigar. Place cabbage stems on bottom of kettle. Arrange cabbage rolls on top, alternating in opposite directions. Add salt and garlic. Press with inverted dish and add water to reach dish. Cover kettle and cook on medium fire 45 minutes. Add lemon juice and cook 10 minutes more.

STUFFING:

    1/2 cup chick-peas
    1 teaspoon oil
    1 cup rice (or cracked wheat #3)
    1/2 bunch minced parsley
    Salt and pepper to taste
    Pinch of cinnamon, nutmeg, allspice

Soak chick-peas overnight. Following day remove from water and rub peas with fingers to remove outer skins. Mix peas with rest of ingredients. *Serves 4.*

FRIED CAULIFLOWER and POTATOES *Zahra wa batata miqlee*

1 cauliflower	2 potatoes, sliced
1 onion, sliced	Oil

Separate cauliflower into flowerets with stems. Fry in hot oil. Place on paper towel to absorb excess oil. Fry onion and potato slices in same oil. Serve with *tahini* sauce and as a side dish with Fish. *Serves 4.*

CAULIFLOWER STEMS *Qarnabeet*

1 pound tender cauliflower stems	1/2 cup chick-peas
1 onion, chopped	1 cup water
1 clove garlic, chopped	Salt to taste
Oil	Juice of 2 lemons

Cut stems into 1-inch pieces and wash thoroughly. Saute onion and garlic in oil. Add chick-peas and simmer. Add water and boil until chick-peas are done, about 30 minutes. In another pan cook stems until tender, about 20 minutes. Remove from water and add to chick-peas. Cook on low fire for a few minutes. Add salt and lemon juice. Serve cold. *Serves 4.*

COOKED DANDELION GREENS *Hindbee mut-bookh*

1 pound dandelion greens	Salt and pepper to taste
2 medium onions, minced	Lemon slices
2 tablespoons olive oil	

Brown onions in oil. Mix in fresh dandelion greens. Toss until all greens are flavored with oil. Cover and steam on low fire until greens are cooked, about 15 minutes. Serve hot or cold, garnished with lemon slices. *Serves 4.*

STEWED EGGPLANT *Imnazelee or Tabakh roohoo* (known to many as "Ratatoule"). This has been prepared for centuries by Middle Eastern people - nutritious and easy-to make.

1/2 cup chick-peas, dry	2 green squash, cubed
1/2 teaspoon baking soda	1 eggplant, cubed
1 clove garlic, chopped	1 large can tomatoes
1 onion, chopped	Salt and pepper to taste
1/3 cup olive oil	

Soak chick-peas with baking soda in water overnight. Following day drain. Remove skins by rubbing peas between fingers. Saute garlic and onion in olive oil. Add chick-peas, cover, and simmer about 15 minutes. Add unpeeled squash, eggplant, and tomatoes. Cover and cook on medium fire until vegetables are tender, about 30 minutes. Serve hot or cold. *Serves 6.*

LENTEN STUFFED GRAPE LEAVES *Waraq 'inib Syamee*

40 grape leaves
1 cup cracked wheat, #2
1/2 cup canned chick-peas (2 oz. can)
1/2 bunch parsley, minced
Salt and pepper to taste
1/4 cup lemon juice

Soak grape leaves in hot water 15 minutes to soften. Remove from water and stem each. Combine wheat, chick-peas, parsley and seasoning. Put 1 teaspoon of stuffing on each leaf and roll. Arrange in rows in pan, each row in opposite directions. Add 1 tablespoon salt. Press stuffed leaves with inverted dish. Add water to reach dish. Cover pan and cook for 35 minutes on medium fire. Add lemon juice and cook another 10 minutes. *Serves 4. 10 per person.*

OKRA STEW *Baymee syamee*

1 pound okra
Juice of 1/2 lemon
2 onions, chopped
1/2 cup olive oil
1 cup stewed tomatoes
1 cup water
2 tablespoons chopped parsley (or cilentro)
Salt and pepper to taste

Wash and carefully trim okra not too close to the top. Sprinkle well with lemon juice and let stand for 20 minutes. Prepare sauce by frying onions lightly in olive oil. Add tomatoes and water. Add parsley and simmer a little longer. Put half the tomato sauce on the bottom of a casserole, drain okra and put on top of sauce. Cover with remaining sauce, season, cover, and simmer gently or bake in slow 300° oven about 30 minutes until okra is tender. *Serves 4.*

SYRIAN MASHED POTATOES *Batata 'arabee mum-ou-sa*

4 medium potatoes
1 onion, diced
1/4 cup oil
Salt and pepper to taste
Juice of 1 lemon
1 onion, sliced
1/2 cup pine nuts

Boil potatoes. Peel and mash. Add diced onion, oil, salt, pepper, and lemon juice and knead together. Fry onions and pine nuts in oil and use to garnish potatoes. *Serves 4.*

RICE AND SPINACH *Roz ma' sabanigh*

1 large onion
1/2 cup oil
2 pounds spinach
3 cups rice
Salt and pepper to taste
6 cups boiling water

Dice onion and brown in oil. Wash spinach and cut in small pieces. Add onion and oil to spinach and cook. Rinse rice, add to spinach, stir well with salt and pepper to taste. Then pour water over the whole. Cook on medium fire for 10 minutes, then on low fire for 15 minutes. *Serves 6.*

COOKED SPINACH *Sabanigh imqala*

2 onions, julienned
1/3 cup olive oil
1 pound spinach, chopped
Salt and pepper to taste
1/4 cup pine nuts
1/4 cup pomegranate seeds (optional)
Lemon wedges

Saute onions in olive oil until translucent. Add spinach, salt, and pepper. Cook on low fire until spinach is cooked, about 20 minutes. Garnish with pine nuts browned in oil. Sprinkle pomegranate seeds on top and edge platter with lemon wedges. *Serves 4.*

FRIED SQUASH *Koosa miqlee*

Wash green squash. Slice. Salt and let stand for 30 minutes. Dredge with flour and fry in hot oil until golden brown. Drain on paper towels. Serve with *tahini* sauce. NOTE: This is delicious served in pocket bread with yogurt cheese, slice of tomato, and onion.

BAKED VEGETABLE DINNER *Aklat khuthra makhbooz*

1 pound each of okra, squash, potatoes, tomatoes, onions
1/4 cup chopped parsley
1/2 cup olive oil
Salt and pepper to taste

Peel potatoes. Slice all vegetables and arrange in baking pan, sprinkling parsley, olive oil, salt and pepper between layers. Add a little water; bake in moderately hot oven (350°) for 1 hour. *Serves 10.*

WHEAT AND TOMATOES

Tabeekh or Burghul ala banadoora

1/2 cup chick-peas (optional)
1/2 teaspoon baking soda
1 onion, chopped
Olive oil
1 cup cracked wheat, #3
1 12-oz. can tomato puree
2 cups boiling water
Salt and pepper to taste
1/2 teaspoon cruched hot pepper (optional)

Soak peas with soda overnight. Following day drain. Remove skins by rubbing peas between fingers. Saute onion in olive oil. Add peas, cover, and simmer about 5 minutes. Add wheat, hot pepper and cook, stirring occasionally, for 2 minutes over medium fire. Add tomato puree and boiling water. Cook on low fire for 20 minutes or until water is absorbed. Add salt and pepper. *Serves 4.*

WHEAT AND CHICK PEAS *Burghul bi Dfeen*

Same as preceding recipe, omitting tomatoes, and include chick peas.

ZANAKER (Meatless kibby)

1 cup cracked wheat, fine
1 medium onion, grated
1/4 cup flour

1/8 cup cold water
Salt and pepper to taste
Yogurt Sauce (see index)

Rinse wheat several times. Squeeze out moisture by cupping hands. Mix thoroughly with onion, flour, water, salt and pepper. Roll into little balls about 1-1/2" in diameter. Drop round balls into Yogurt sauce and cook for 20 minutes. *Serves 3. Serve with a salad.*

MUNSOOFEE (lenten wheat dish)

1 cup cracked wheat, fine
1 medium onion, julienned
1/4 cup flour

1/8 cup cold water
Salt and pepper to taste
Sumac or lemon juice

Rinse wheat several times. Squeeze out moisture by cupping hands. Mix together the wheat, flour, water, salt and pepper. Flatten into 3 inches in diameter rounds. Saute onion in a little oil. Add rounds of wheat on top of onions Add a small amount of water. Sprinkle sumac on top of the wheat rounds. If sumac is not available, use lemon juice. Cover and let steam for 20 minutes. *Serves 4.*

RICE with FAVA BEANS *Roz ma' ful*

1 large onion, chopped
3 tablespoons olive oil
1 pound fresh shelled fava beans
1 teaspoon salt

1/2 teaspoon pepper
4 sprigs cilentro *(kizbara)*
2 cups long grain rice

In saucepan, saute onion in oil until translucent. Add fava beans and saute a few minutes, stirring gently. Cover with 1/4 cup water, salt and pepper. In skillet, saute cilentro in 2 tablespoons oil. Rinse and drain rice. Add rice to cilentro and saute a few minutes. Add the rice-cilentro mixture to the fava beans. Add 4 cups boiling water. Cover, bring to a boil, then simmer gently for about 20 minutes until all water is absorbed.

BAKED POTATOES AND ONIONS. (This is another tasty lenten meal prepared with a tomato sauce.) See recipe on page 34 and omit the lamb. Serve with hot *talamee* (round thick bread) and a salad.

FOR ADDITIONAL LENTEN FOODS, SEE VEGETABLE CHAPTER, PAGE 59. Many of these recipes can be prepared without meat.

Helen fills dessert plates with qroon, some of many pastries she prepared at the Indianapolis Press Club for gubernatorial fund-raiser dinner party

LENTEN DESSERTS

Hiloo Syamee

LENTEN CAKES *Karabeej Syamee or Qroon*

- 3 cups flour
- 2/3 cup oil
- 1/2 cup sugar
- 1 teaspoon anise seeds
- 1 teaspoon *mahleb* crushed
- 1/2 cup warm water

Combine ingredients and knead well. Cut dough into small patties. Flatten patties in palm of hand to 2-1/2 inches in diameter. Fill with 1 tablespoon filling and crimp edges together in crescent shape. Bake in 350° moderate oven until bottoms are lightly browned. Place under broiler until tops are lightly browned. Let cool, then dip in syrup.

FILLING: Combine the following:

- 2 cups ground English walnuts
- 1/4 cup sugar
- 1 tablespoon orange-blossom water

SYRUP: Same as Baklawa syrup. See index. *Yield: 50 cakes.*

TURKISH DELIGHT *Laqoum or Tutlee*

- 3 tablespoons gelatin
- 1/2 cup cold water
- 2 cups sugar
- 1/2 cup hot water
- Grated rind and juice of 2 lemons
- Grated rind and juice of 1 orange
- Red or green food coloring
- 1/2 pound pistachio nuts, chopped
- Confectioner's sugar

Soften gelatin in cold water. Combine sugar and hot water and heat to boiling. Add gelatin and simmer 20 minutes. Add citrus juices, rind and coloring. Strain into loaf pan. The pan should be large enough so the mixture is 1/2 to 1 inch deep. Add chopped nuts. Chill until firm. When cold, cut into cubes and roll in confectioners' sugar. *Yield: 2 dozen.*

ANISE-DATE CRESCENTS *Qroon ajwat yansoon - Macaroon* (this recipe is time-consuming, but the end results are worth the effort. Every bite calls for another one).

6 cups flour
1/2 cup sugar
1/2 teaspoon salt
1 box (1-1/2 oz. whole anise seed

1/2 cup sesame seeds
1-2/3 cup corn oil
1/4 cup or more warm water

Mix together all dry ingredients. Add oil, rubbing through the dry ingredients thoroughly worked through. Then add 1/4 cup water, kneading dough to a pliable consistency, adding more water if necessary. The dough will not be as soft as a bread dough. Knead well. Set aside and cover with wax paper for 1/2 hour. *Note: No yeast in this dough.*

Mix together the following ingredients and set to one side:

2 pounds pitted dates, minced fine - 1/2 pound shelled nut meats, walnut or pecan.

Make Baklawa syrup, page 99. Set to one side to cool.

Preheat oven to 350°. Make round balls of dough the size of a golf ball. Place ball in palm of hand. Flatten dough with index finger of right hand. Fill with date/nut mixture and close to form a crescent, pinching edges together. Place crescents on ungreased baking sheets. Bake for approximately 20 minutes. Broil until light brown. *Yield: 125.*
As soon as crescents are baked, remove from oven and dip in cooled syrup. Place on rack to drain. These keep well in the freezer. Defrost in 10 minutes and ready to serve guests.

SESAME SEED PIE *Fatayer Simsum*

Lenten Pie Dough , page 117
1 cup sesame seeds

1/2 cup sugar
Oil

Mix sesame seeds and sugar with just enough oil to hold mix together. Place on dough, open face, 3 inches in diameter. Bake in 350° oven for 15 minutes; then place under broiler 30 seconds until lightly golden. *Yield: 3 dozen pies.*

BARLEY, BOILED. Especially in the winter-time, this nutritious and tasty dessert is enjoyed by both adults and children (see page 137).

MEATLESS MENUS

For those of you abstaining from meat, you'll find an infinite variety of enticing healthy foods in the various chapters for your eating pleasure. To assist you, turn to Chapters on Lenten foods - Fish - Breads and Pies with nutritious fillings of chick peas, spinach, thyme - yogurt cheese and vegetables filled with cracked wheat or rice-chick pea fillings. Mounds of grapes and all kinds of fresh fruit is always an excellent choice for dessert. A treat for adults and children is the Boiled barley with raisins, the anise bread - and known to many of you as "Elephant Ears", our similar but tastier Zalabee and Awam.

Here are a few suggested menus:

Cracked Wheat and Tomatoes	126
Cauliflower and Potatoes	124
Chick pea pies	117
Pickled vegetables	74
Mra-qud bread	80
Green bean stew	123
Rice with orzo	46
Syrian bread salad	22
Marquq bread	78
Lenten stuffed grape leaves	125
Potato kibby	119
Pickled turnips	73
Zalabee	140
Rice with fava beans	127
Eggplant and cheese	124
Fatayer za'tar	118
Baked vegetable dinner	126
Spinach pies	118
Boiled barley	137
Lentil-Wheat Soup	12
Wheat garden salad	18
Awam	140
Baked potatoes and onions	127
Eggplant stew	63
Syrian bun-type bread	80
Fried cauliflower	124
Tahini	4
Fish kibby	113
Lentil salad	21

Parishioners of St. George Orthodox Church, Indianapolis, partake of the Holy Eucharist from the Parish Priest Reverend Nabil Hanna and His Grace Bishop Demetri of the Toledo Archdiocese.

Holy Oblation
Prosphoron or Qurban
—recipe on page 133

TRADITIONS AND FOODS OF THE ORTHODOX CATHOLIC CHURCH

HOLY ALTAR BREAD *Prosphoron or Qurban*

Holy Communion is observed every Sunday in the Eastern Orthodox Catholic Church. In this service the sacraments of the Eucharist are bread and wine. The priest commemorates the Last Supper, saying: "He took bread, and gave thanks and broke it, and gave unto them saying, Take eat, this is my body which is broken for you; this do in remembrance of me." **(Luke 22:19)**

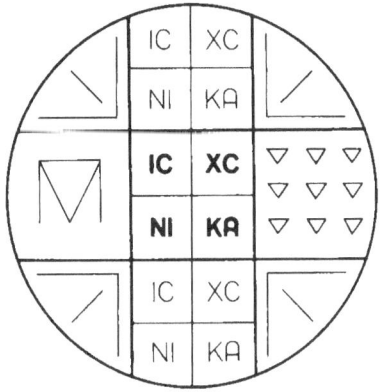

The wine, having the color of blood, is from the pure juice of the vine. The bread, which must be leavened, is from clean wheat. **(Cor. 5:7,8)**. It is baked in a flat, round loaf called *Prosphoron* **(Greek)** or *Qurban (Arabic)*, and is stamped with a seal.

#1. Maheeba holding seal for stamping dough

In the Holy Communion service, five loaves commemorate the loaves with which the Lord satisfied five thousand souls. **(Matt. 14:15-21)** Each loaf (called oblation) has been stamped with the seal.

In the center portion of each loaf is impressed the sign of the Cross, surrounded by the **Greek** letters IC (meaning Jesus), XC (meaning Christ), and the word NIKA (meaning conquer). This center portion is called the Lamb in memory of Christ.

#2. Stamping the dough

The priest removes the center portion from the first loaf and places it on the paten.

From the second loaf he removes the large triangular piece in honor of the Blessed Virgin and places it on the paten. From the third loaf he removes the nine smaller triangular pieces in commemoration of the Angelic Hosts and the Saints of the Orthodox Church, and also places them on the paten. From the fourth, parts are taken for the living, and from the fifth, parts are taken for the dead.

The priest partakes of the Holy Communion (bread and wine) and these sacraments are then given to parishioners during the

#3. Placing small holes in dough

divine liturgy. Prior to church services, the applicants confess their sins to the priest. During the service they walk with bowed head toward the church altar where the priest stands holding the sacred chalice. The applicant holds under his chin the silk napkin hanging from the priest's hand to make sure that no part of the sacrament falls on the floor. The priest dips a small golden spoon into the chalice containing the divine sacraments of the Last Supper and administers it to the lips of the parishioner. In the background the choir can be heard singing the communion hymn, "Receive Ye the Body of Christ."

Following the divine liturgy, the priest distributes the remaining portions of the *Qurban* to the parishioners. This Holy Oblation is prepared by Orthodox families wishing to remember a loved one; prayers are said by the priest during services for all members of the family, living and deceased.

- 2 packages dry yeast
- 5 pounds flour
- 2 teaspoons salt
- 1 teaspoon sugar
- 1 teaspoon crushed *mahleb* (optional)
- Warm water
- Holy stamp

Dissolve yeast in 1/4 cup warm water with sugar. Pour flour, salt and *mahleb* in pan. Add dissolved yeast and approximately 6 cups warm water to the flour mixture. Knead, turning over until smooth. Cover with cloth and plastic and set in warm place about 1-1/2 to 2 hours. Roll between cupped hands until smooth. Cover with cloth and plastic. This will prevent dough from drying.

Flatten each ball of dough with hands to 1/4-inch thickness. Allow to set for another hour, covering again with cloth and plastic. Preheat oven to 400°. Stamp each loaf in center with Holy Stamp and make five holes around loaf about 1 inch from edge of seal. This will prevent rising. Bake in oven until bottoms become light brown. Remove from oven and brush face of *Qurban* with cold water. Broil until loaves are light brown. NOTE: The Holy Stamp may be purchased from stores listed in Shopper's Guide.

EASTER EGGS *Bythet il 'Eed*

Most of us take Easter eggs for granted, boiling and coloring them, giving them to relatives and friends, hiding them for the children to hunt down. The real meaning of the Easter egg, however, is often overlooked.

*One of the earliest religious uses of the egg was by the Egyptians in worshipping Ra. As a symbol of fertility and of renewed life among the ancient **Egyptians and Persians,** the egg was customarily colored during spring festivities. The Egyptians colored the eggs red to represent the sun; the shell represented the earth, and the white of the egg represented heaven.

The egg is also a symbol of the Resurrection of Christ, since it has new life within its walls. Among Christians, the Easter egg represents the sealed tomb in which the body of Christ was placed after His crucifixion; the shell being the sealed tomb having dormant life inside.

During the early days of Christianity only red - signifying the blood of Christ - was used to color the eggs. Other colors however, are commonly used today, such as white, ivory, and tan to represent the fine linen cloth in which Christ's body was wrapped before it was placed in the sepulchre. Green represents the vegetation of the springtime - the awakening of the earth from the deep slumber of winter. Blue represents the blue of the sky - the peace and joy of the Easter season. Yellow represents the early morning starlight of the resurrection. Purple represents the passion of the crucified Christ and the joy of the resurrected Christ. Multicolored eggs represent the time when Jesus gave up the ghost. Sweet-smelling essences, traditionally mixed with the colorings, are in remembrance of the ointment-bearing women who, early on the first Easter morning, went to annoint the body of Christ with rich spices and perfumes. *Adapted from writings of Reverend Elias G. Karim, Oklahoma City, Oklahoma.

For Easter, Syrian and Lebanese children gather vegetable roots, onion and pomegranate skins to make coloring for the eggs, which are taken to church and blessed by the priest. Then they are distributed among the parishioners after services on the eve of Easter. Not only in Syria and Lebanon, but also in America and throughout the world, these same impressive services prevail in Orthodox Catholic churches. During the service, the congregation follows the priest three times around the inside of the church; each person carries a lighted candle. Everyone leaves the church except a man, representing Satan, who stands in the dark behind the closed door to prevent the priest from entering. The priest, representing Christ, approaches the closed door and chants for the doors to be opened that the King of Glory may enter. The chanting is repeated 3 times, and Satan vanishes. The priest throws open the door to symbolize the victory of Christ over Satan. The church is immediately illuminated and the multitude follow the priest singing the message of resurrection *"Al Maseeh Qam"* in **Arabic** *"Kristos anasti"* in **Greek,** and "Christ is Risen" in **English.** After the service, the fast is broken with an Easter egg, a bowl of Chicken-Rice Soup, and a sweet dessert of Rice-Custard.

At the conclusion of the divine liturgy in the Orthodox Church, the eggs are blessed and distributed among the congregation by the priest. Members of the congregation then greet each other and hit the eggs together to signify the breaking of Christ's tomb. Eating eggs at Easter is symbolic of breaking fast, since eggs are forbidden during Lent.

All eggs of the feast should be broken to show that Christ has conquered death and has risen, thereby granting new life to all who believe in Him.

After having abstained from meats and dairy products during the Great Lent, everyone looks forward to Easter dinner. Days of preparation have been spent in baking pastries and bread, rolling grape leaves, coring squash, and paring eggplant. Following the dinner, an assortment of pastries is served to guests along with Turkish coffee, and, of course, the colorful *Bythet il Eed* (easter egg).

NOTE: In celebrating the feast of the resurrection, the feast is not a calendar date, but the time is regulated by the first full moon of the vernal equinox and the first full moon following the Jewish passover.

BOILED WHEAT FOR REQUIEM LITURGY *Qilbee or Ruhmee*

An old rite of the Orthodox Catholic Church is the requiem liturgy. In this service it is customary to distribute portions of *Qilbee* (cooked whole wheat) in memory of the deceased on the fortieth day after a death, as well as on the first anniversary.

The boiled wheat symbolizes the resurrection. The Lord said "Verily, verily, I say unto you, except a corn of wheat fall into the ground and die, it abideth alone; but if it die, it bringeth forth much fruit" (**John 12:24**). Sugar added to the *qilbee* indicates the sweetness everlasting life.

Today in America, as well as in parts of Europe and the Middle East, the wheat offering in church by the family of the deceased symbolizes the act of charity.

5 pounds whole wheat	1 box powdered sugar
4 cups chopped walnuts	3 oz. silver dragees
2-1/2 cups granulated sugar	1 pound candy-coated almonds
4 teaspoons cinnamon	
3 boxes raisins	

Pour wheat in large kettle and cover with water. Allow to stand overnight. In the morning, drain and cover with fresh water. Cook about 4 hours or until tender. Stir often with wooden spoon to keep from sticking. Drain and spread on a large cloth to absorb excess moisture. Mix with walnuts, sugar, cinnamon, and raisins. Mound slightly on serving trays lined with wax paper and edged with paper doilies. Sprinkle powdered sugar over top and press down with wax paper to make a smooth compact top. Cut out a large cardboard cross and make an impression with it in sugar. Fill space with the silver dragees. On either side of the cross, form initials of the deceased with raisins. Border the tray with almonds. *Yield: 1 medium and 1 small serving tray.*

FEASTS

<u>EASTER.</u> THE FEAST OF CHRIST'S RESURRECTION, HOLY EASTER, IS THE <u>MAJOR FEAST OF THE CHURCH</u>

<u>The Twelve Great Feasts.</u> The eight Great Feasts in honor of Christ and the four Great Feasts in honor of His Mother are called the Twelve Great Feasts.

September 8. The Nativity of the Theotokos.
September 14. The Elevation of the Holy Cross.
November 21. The Presentation of the Theotokos.
December 25. Christmas (the nativity of Christ).
January 6. Epiphany (the baptism of Christ).
February 2. The Presentation of the Lord.
March 25. The Annunciation.
The Sunday before Easter - Palm Sunday
Forty Days after Easter - The Ascension of the Lord
Fifty Days after Easter - Pentecost.
August 6. The Transfiguration.
August 15. The Falling Asleep of the Theotokos.

MARCH 25 FEAST DAY

March 25th is the feast day of the Annunciation of the Virgin Mary in the Orthodox Catholic Church. Traditionally, sea foods are eaten on this day. A traditional menu:

Shrimp cocktail - Hot red mullets - Anchovy fillets
Spinach pies - Thyme-sumac pies
Syrian potato salad
Arabic coffee - Lenten cakes

AUGUST 6 FEAST DAY

The feast day of the Transfiguration of Christ is celebrated on the sixth day of August in the Orthodox Catholic Church. Although this day falls in the fifteen-day Lenten period of August 1-15, because it is a feast day of the Church, a concession is made and fish is the accepted meal of the day.

Baked Fish - Sesame oil with lemon
Fried squash - Fried tomatoes - Salad
Talamee (Syrian bun-type bread)   Fruit

AUGUST 15 FEAST DAY

August 15 marks the feast of the Assumption of the Virgin Mary in the Orthodox Catholic Church. This feast day is the termination of the fifteen-day Lenten period.

Baked Chicken - Rice-Hashwa dressing
Raw Kibby - Baked eggplant - Meat Pies
Salad - Coffee - Pudding

BOILED BARLEY *'I-youq - Sleeqa*

I-youq is served on the feast day of St. Barbara, which falls on December 4. The feast day of St Barbara commemorates the third century martyr who died by her father's hand rather than renounce her belief in Christ.

1 cup yellow barley
1 teaspoon anise seed
1 cup raisins

1/2 cup English walnuts
Sugar

Cook barley in quart of water in covered pan on low fire for 2-1/2 hours, adding more water during cooking. Stir occasionally to keep from sticking. Add raisins and anise seeds. Simmer 10 more minutes. Add a teaspoon of sugar in each bowl before eating. Garnish with english walnuts.

Written in Arabic, Jesus feeds the multitudes with 5 loaves of bread. Background of photo is the traditional *Awam* and *Zalabee* served during the Feast of Epiphany. *(Matt. 14:15-21)*

Reverend Anthony Yazge dips brush in Holy Water for the blessing of our home during the Feast of Epiphany. The water is sprinkled throughout all of the rooms in the home as the Baptismal chant is repeated. Prayers were said by my mother *Maheeba* and brother Bob. The tradition lives on as we serve *Zalabee* and *Awam* following the blessing of the home. This typifies the blessing received in every Antiochian Orthodox home during the celebration of the **Feast of Epiphany.**

THE FEAST OF EPIPHANY

(Mark 1:9 - Matt. 28-19)

El-Gitas

Frying Zalabee for Feast of Epiphany

Epiphany, considered one of the oldest and most important festivals of the Christian Church, is celebrated on the twelfth day after Christmas. Families spend the morning at the many cathedrals in Damascus and Beirut. Processions of worshippers can be seen walking to the cathedrals to seek comfort and redemption on this day of Epiphany in commemoration of the baptism of Jesus in the Jordan River. **(Mark 1:19)** The interiors of the Orthodox Catholic cathedrals show beautiful Byzantine artwork in the Icons that surround the Royal Door of the church altar. Following church services, the priests visit the homes of their parishioners and bless the corners of all the rooms of the house with holy water. Before they leave, the traditional material feast of *Zalabee and Awam* is served.

We've all learned from my mother of her activites in Syria the day before Epiphany when she helped her mother in preparing *Zalabee and Awam*. And the tradition lives on as we all continue to make these doughnut-shaped cakes. Fried in oil, when cooled, they are sprinkled with sugar to signify sweet and everlasting life. Although today's method for making them has been simplified, at one time the dough used for the cakes was the result of being "baptized". The ceremony for the baptizing of the dough began with tying the dough in a white cloth. It was then carried to a fountain, immersed in the name of the Holy Trinity, and the baptismal chant repeated. The dough in the white cloth hung in the tree for 3 days, then was taken in the house. The dough rose without yeast. This new leaven, miraculously raised, provided the yeast for the next year. From this dough, small crosses were made and placed where food was stored in the dwelling.

In America, following evening Epiphany services in the Orthodox Catholic Church, parishioners gather in the church hall to partake of *Zalabee and Awam* prepared by members of the church. During the week of Epiphany, the priest visits all the homes of parishioners to bless them with holy water.

DOUGHNUT CAKES *Zalabee* (similar to elephant ears at many food fairs - these are even better)

4 cups flour	**1 tablespoon oil**
1 package dry yeast	**Warm water**
1 teaspoon sugar	**Granulated sugar**
1 teaspoon salt	**Cinnamon**

Mix yeast with water and sugar to proof. Add to the flour, salt, oil and water, kneading until mixture is soft. Cover dough until it rises, about 1 hour. Cut in strips 2" wide, about 7" long. Fry in skillet of hot oil until golden brown. Remove from skillet. Place on absorbent paper to remove excess oil. Sprinkle with sugar/cinnamon mixture. *Yield: 12.*
Fast method: Open a can of biscuits, pat out the biscuits, rest for 10 minutes, fry in oil and top with sugar.

SPOON DOUGHNUTS *Awam*

2 medium potatoes	**1 package dry yeast**
2 cups flour	**Warm water**

Peel potatoes, cube, and boil. Remove from water and mash. Add flour, yeast and water. Knead, leaving mixture soft. Set until dough rises, about 1 hour. Pick up small portions of dough with a spoon and drop in skillet of hot oil until browned. Remove and dip in cold syrup. Use same syrup as Baklawa syrup (pg. 99). *Yield: 2 dozen.*

Family involvement at the festival. Never too young - Godchild Alexis Azar kneads another batch of dough. Sister Kate Malooley and Grandma to Alexis, stretches dough for frying. Alexis' mother Cathy fries the dough and then mixes it in a cinnamon/sugar mix.

GLOSSARY

Qa-moos

Syrians and Lebanese speak the Arabic language. In spelling the Arabic names, I have tried to present phonetically each word in acceptable Arabic.

One of the richest languages in the world, Arabic has full vowels, pronounced as follows: the a in the word *baqdownas* is pronounced like the *a* in the word "daughter". Arabic-speaking people differ as to the best spelling of Arabic names in English. *Baqdownas* (parsley) may also be properly pronounced *ba'downas*. Just as pronunciation differs from Boston to Birmingham in America, so Arabic dialects change from village to village and the various countries of the Middle East. A small number of sibilants produce a hissing sound as in *sittee* (Grandmother). The vowel *u* is pronounced as in "bus" or *bus-il* (onions). The *q* in *baqdownas* and *gh* in *ghanum* (lamb) are pronounced with a gutteral sound produced by a contraction of the larynx. The *r* is always rolled.

I hope you will find entertainment in adding these words and phrases to your Arabic vocabulary.

Pertaining to Food and Drinks

Ad-dis	Lentils
Ah-jeen	Dough
Ah-sal	Honey
Ah-seer il li-moon	Lemon juice
A-raq	Anise-flavored liqueur
Baqdownas	Parsley
Banadoora	Tomato
Ba-tinjan	Eggplant
Bay-mee	Okra
Bhar hub wa na'im	Allspice
Booza	Ice Cream
Burghul	Wheat, crushed
Bus-il	Onion
By-thet il Eed	Easter eggs
By-thot	Eggs
Dib-s	Molasses
Djaj	Chicken
Fatayer	Pies (turnovers)
Fil-ful	Pepper
Fis-duq	Pistachio
Ful	Beans, fava (or broad)

Fo-tir	Mushrooms
Gha-num	Lamb
Gri-bee	Cookies, butter
Ha-beq or *Num-name*	Basil, sweet
Ha-leeb	Milk
Hind-bee	Dandelion
Ho-mos	Chick-Peas
Hub il hal	Cardamon
Hub-et il baraky	Caraway, black
'I-jee	Omelet
'Inib	Grapes
In-jas	Pears
Ji-zar	Carrot
Jo-ban	Cheese
Jun-za-beel	Ginger
Ka-ick	Anise bread
Ka-moun	Cumin powder
Kha-roof	Sheep
Kho-baz	Bread
Khus	Lettuce
Khyar	Cucumber
Kizbara	Coriander or Cilentro
Koosa	Squash
Khuthra	Vegetables
Laban	Yogurt
La-hum	Meat
Lahum buqqar	Beef
Lahum 'ijil	Veal
Lahum khun-zeer	Pork
Lift	Turnip
Lowz	Almonds
Lu-bee	Beans, green
Mah-leb	Cherry kernels, black
Mar-da-koosh	Marjoram
Mar-qeh	Sauce
Ma-warid	Rose water
Ma-za-har	Orange-blossom water
Mi-leh	Salt
Mul-foof	Cabbage
My	Water
Na'na	Mint
Nbeeth	Wine
Qah-weh	Coffee
Qa-mar-deen	Dried apricot leather

Qa-tar	Syrup
Qum-eh	Whole wheat
Qurban	Holy bread
Ra-man	Pomegranate
Roz	Rice
Sa-ba-nigh	Spinach
Sa-far-jel	Quince
Salata	Salad
Sa-mek	Fish
Sa-min	Butter
Sfee-ha	Meat pies
Sha-hum khun-zeer	Bacon
Sha-mun-der	Beets
Sha'-ree-yee	Orzo or Rosa Marina
Shou-ra-ba	Soup
Shraab	Fruit juices
Shy	Tea
Si-kar	Sugar
Sim-sum	Sesame seeds
Snoo-ber	Pine nuts
Ta-fah	Apples
T-heen	Flour
Thi-ra	Corn
Thume	Garlic
Waraq il gar	Bay leaf
Yansoon	Anise seeds
Yukh-nee	Stew
Zahra	Cauliflower
Za'tar	Blend of thyme and sumac
Zbeeb	Raisins
Zite	Oil
Zi-toon	Olives

RELATING TO RELIGION

Allah	God
Ba-khoor	Incense
Eed il faseh or Eed il Kbeer	Easter
Eed il Meelad	Christmas
El Gi-tas	Epiphany
Il Ab	The Father
Il Ibn	The Son
Il Rooh il Qo-dos	The Holy Ghost
Il Tha-looth	The Trinity

Il Kotab il Mooqadas	The Holy Scriptures
Il Ma-za-meer	The Psalms
Il Ra-say-il	The Epistles
Il Sa-boo il a-lum	Passion week
Il Sa-lot il Rubaneeyet	Lord's Prayer
Il Syam	Lent
Il Too-rot	The Bible
Il Un-jeel	The Gospel
Kas	Chalice
Knee-set	Church
Mab-kha-rut	Censer
Ma-lake	Angel
Mariam il Ath-ra	The Virgin Mary
Moo-kha-lis	Saviour
Mus-be-hut	Rosary
Na-bee	Prophet
Ra-sool	Apostle
Qa-dees	Saint
Sa-leeb	Cross
Tir-tee-let	Hymn
Ya-soo' il Ma-seeh	Jesus Christ

RECIPE INDEX

Note: * additional recipes for Party Servings

Appetizers
    Chick-pea Sesame Dip* 4
    Cottage cheese balls 3
    Cheese with junket 2
    Cottage cheese with lemon 2
    Eggplant with laban 3
    Eggplant with sesame oil 5
    Homos bi tahini 4
    Raw Beef 1
    Spanakopeta 3
    Spinach Fillo Triangles 3
    Tahini with laban 5
    Tahini - Taratoor 4
    Yogurt balls 3
    Yogurt cheese 2
    Za'tar chips 5

Bedouin Feast (Mansef) 29

Beverages, 87
    Anise tea 89
    Apricot drink 89
    Cinnamon tea 89
    Helen's Sun Tea 89
    Lemonade 90
    Mulberry drink 88
    Spice drink 89
    Turkish coffee 88
    Wine 90

Breads and Pies, 77
    Anise bread* 81
    Basic pie dough 82
    Braided egg bread (Challah) 86
    Cheese pies 84
    Kishik pies 84
    Khobaz Smeek (skillet bread) 84

Meat pies* 83
Pecan crusted Cheese pies 84
Pocket bread 80
Potato pies 84
Yogurt-mint pies 85
Yogurt pies* 85
Syrian bread, round-bun type 80
Syrian bread, thin loaves 78
Vegetarian pies 118

Butter, clarified (or rendered) 45

Candied fruits and preserves, 91
    Almond candy 94
    Apricots, sugared 92
    Candied orange, grapefruit,
        lemon peel 94
    Dates, candied 92
    Eggplant, syruped 92
    Fig conserve 93
    Figs, stuffed 93
    Pears, candied 91
    Pears, sugared 92
    Watermelon preserves 94

Couscous 49

Church Traditions and Foods, 133
    Altar bread 134
    Barley, boiled 137
    Easter eggs and service 134
    Feasts 136
    Feast of Epiphany 139
        Doughnut cakes 140
        Spoon doughnuts 141
    Wheat for requiem liturgy 136

Cheese. See Appetizers

Desserts. See Pastries 97

Fasts prescribed by the Holy Eastern
   Orthodox Church 115

Fish, 110
   Baked fish 111
   Baked halibut 111
   Baked stuffed fish 110
   Cod with Sauce 112
   Flounder with Mushroom sauce 112
   Hot red mullets 112
   Fisherman's Stew 114
   Kibby samek 113
   Oysters baked with sauce 113
   Red snapper 110
   Samke Harra (Fish w/Hot Sauce) 113
   Shrimp cocktail sauce 113
   Trout, grilled 111
   Trout, pan fried 114

Game, Poultry and Dressings, 41
   Chicken, marinated and broiled 43
   Chicken with okra 44
   Chicken roast 42
   Chicken stew 44
   Chicken with Sumac 44
   Chicken with rice-walnut stuffing 42
   Duck with wine sauce 42
   Giblet-bread stuffing 45
   Goose, roast 42
   Minced lamb-rice dressing 45
   Pheasant, roast 41
   Rabbit, fried 43
   Rice-orzo dressing* 46
   Rice-giblet dressing 47
   Turkey 43

Kibby, 51
   Baked 55
   Baked, football shape 54
   Fried 54
   Kibby patties with turkey 54
   Raw Kibby 52

   With kishik sauce 55
   With laban and walnuts 54
   With yogurt-rice sauce 55

Lenten foods and menus 115

Lenten desserts, 129
   Anise-date crescents 130
   Lenten cakes 129
   Sesame candy 107
   Turkish delight 129
   Barley, boiled 137

Lenten Kibby and Falafel, 119
   Fish Kibby 113
   Fried potato Kibby 119
   Meatless Kibby 127
   Potato Kibby 119
   Pumpkim Kibby 120
   Falafel 120

Lenten Menus 136

Lenten Pies, 117
   Chick-pea pie 117
   Dough, Lenten pie 117
   Sesame-seed pie 130
   Spinach pie 118
   Thyme-sumac pie 118

Lenten salads (See salad section) 17

Lenten Wheat and Vegetables, 123-127
   Cabbage rolls 123
   Cauliflower, fried 124
   Cauliflower, stems 124
   Cracked wheat and tomatoes 126
   Dandelion greens, cooked 124
   Eggplant, stewed 124
   Fava beans 60
   Grape leaves, stuffed 125
   Green bean stew 123
   Potatoes, mashed 125

Rice and spinach 125
Spinach, cooked 126
Squash, fried 126
Vegetable dinner, baked 126
Okra Stew 125

Lenten lentil dishes, 121
Lentil-potato soup 121
Lentils and rice 122
Lentils with tomatoes 122
Lentils and wheat 121
Noodles and lentils 122
Strained lentils 121
Mansef 29

Meats, 31
Baby lamb roast 37
Beef tongue, boiled 33
Lamb Casing Sausages 38
Lamb baked with potatoes 34
Lamb breast 37
With rice-nut mixture 37
Lamb burgers 33
Lamb burger with pine nuts 33
Lamb dumplings with yogurt sauce 33
Lamb liver 34
Lamb and mushrooms 34
Lamb on skewers 35
Lamb stew 35
Lamb tripe 35
Lamb with yogurt 36
Meat-egg roll 36
Roast leg of lamb 32
Sheep's kidneys 37
Veal breast 36

Menus, Arabic XVIII

Olives, 25
black 25
green 26

Omelets, 57
Egg omelet 57
Squash 57

Pastries and desserts, 97
Almond rolls 102
Butter cookies 103
Date crescents 105
Fillo bird's nests 101
Galatoboureko 109
Halawa cake 107
Halawa diamonds 107
Milk farina 107
Nut-filled cakes 104
Nut rings 102
Pastry sheets 98
Pastry delights, diamond 98
Pastry delights, sesame 103
Rice custard 106
Ricotta pastries* 100
Sesame cookies 105
Sesame Twist cookies 108
Shredded wheat, stuffed 103
Vanilla pudding 106
Whole wheat (qamheeyee) 106

Pickles, 72
Cucumber 73
Cauliflower, pickled 72
Eggplant, garlic 72
Grapes, spiced 75
Mangoes stuffed with cabbage 74
Mixed vegetables, pickled 74
Onions, pickled 75
Turnips, pickled 73
Squash, canned 76

Pies. See Bread and pies 41

Poultry. See Game, poultry 41

Salads, 17
- Beef tongue salad 19
- Beet salad 20
- Broccoli-Pasta salad 23
- Carrot salad 23
- Chick pea salad 24
- Combination salad 21
- Coucous salad 50
- Cucumber yogurt salad 20
- Dandelion salad 20
- Eggplant salad 21
- Fava bean salad 22
- Lemon Parsley-Walnut salad 19
- Lentil salad 21
- Lima bean salad 22
- Noodle-Cabbage-Almond 24
- Pasta with watercress 24
- Purslane salad 18
- Rice-Pasta salad 23
- Shrimp avocado salad 23
- Spinach salad 19
- Syrian bread salad 22
- Syrian potato salad 23
- Salmon salad 23
- Tomato-sardine salad 23
- Wheat-garden salad (tabooley)* 18

Soups, 11
- Barley soup 12
- Chicken and Matzo Balls 14
- Chicken-rice soup 11
- Chick-pea soup 11
- Chili 15
- Egyptian mlukheeyeh 13
- Kishik soup 9
- Lentil-spinach soup 15
- Lentil-wheat soup 12
- Lentils and wheat with kishik 11
- Lentils with vegetables 122
- Navy bean soup 14
- Vegetable soup 12
- Yogurt-cucumber soup 13

Spices and herbs XV

Vegetables, 59
- Artichokes, stuffed 70
- Beans, fava with cilentro and lamb 60
- Beans, navy 71
- Beans, green 65
- Beans, lima 65
- Broccoli 61
- Cabbage rolls 60
- Cauliflower-rice inverted mold 66
- Eggplant and cheese 63
- Eggplant, stuffed and baked 62
- Eggplant stew 63
- Fava beans with rice 127
- Grape leaf rolls* 63
- Grape leaves, canned and frozen 76
- Lima beans and lamb 65
- Okra 65
- Peppers, stuffed 64
- Rice-eggplant inverted 66
- Squash, stuffed 68
- Squash with yogurt sauce 67
- Squash, canned 76
- Squash, frozen 75
- Swiss chard 61
- Spinach, steamed 66
- Spinach with meat 67
- Squash with tahini-yogurt 70

See Lenten wheat and vegetables 123-127

Wheat and Kibby 7

Yogurt 147

ARABIC INDEX

Addis imquala 121
Addis imsafa 121
Addis ma' banadoora 122
Ahjeen fatayer syam 117
Ahjeen il baklawa 98
Ahjeen il fatayer 82
Akal qumeh wa khuthra 123
Akal syam 115
Aklat addis 121
Aklat khuthra makhbooz 126
Almaseeyee 106
Araq 90
Ardashowki 70
Arnabee miqli 43
Awam 140

Barazek 105
Baba ghanouj 5
Baklawa 98
Baklawa simsum 103
Batata arabee mumousa 125
Batata arabee salata 23
Batinjan bil saneeyee 62
Batinjan imfasakh 3
Batinjan makboos 72
Batinjan makdoos 72
Batinjan ma' good 92
Batinjan wa joban 63
Baymee 65
Baymee syamee 125
Booza sooree 108
Burghul ala banadoora 126
Burghul bi dfeen 127
Burghul wa kibby 51
Busil makboos 75
But ma' marqeh 42
Butteekh mouraba 94
Bythet il Eed 134

Couscous 49

Djaj ma'limoon wa za' tar 43
Djaj mihshee ma' hashwa roz 42
Djaj mishwee 42

El-Gitas 139

Fajoom 65, 71
Fakheth lahum ghanum 32
Falafel 119
Fasoolya ma lahum 65
Fatayer batata 84
Fatayer homos 117
Fatayer laban ma' no'na 85
Fatayer laban ma' qawarma 85
Fatayer sabanigh 118
Fatayer simsum 118
Fatayer syamee 117
Fatayer za'tar 118
Fatoush 22
Fawakee ma' qood wa mourubba 91
Finjan qirfee 89
Flyflee mihshee 64
Fooleeye 60
Ful imdamis 22
Ful-eeyee syamee 60
Fatit il koosa 70

Gambaree ma' marqet 113
Ghanum ma' fotir 34
Ghanum ma' lubee 65
Ghanum ma' nbeeth 35
Ghanum mihshee 37
Gribee 103
Ghumee 35

Habesh 43
Halawa cake 107
Halawa diamonds 107
Halawat eb joban 106
Hashwa ghanum ma' snoober 45
Hashwa qiwanis ma' khobaz 45

Hareesee	12
Hashwa roz	47
Hashwa roz wa jowz	47
Hiloo	97
Hiloo syamee	129
Hilwat ib miskee	93
Hindbee mutbookh	124
Homos bi tahini	4
Ijee	57
Ijet il koosa	57
Imfarakat koosa	57
Imjadara	121
Imjadara ma' roz	122
Imjadara humra	12
Imnazalee	124
Inkha	39
Inib imkhullal	75
Injas ma' sikkar	92
Injas ma' qood	91
Iyouq	137
Joq Mihshee	38
Kafta snoober	33
Ka-ick	81
Karabeej syamee	129
Khobaz arabee	78
Khobaz wa fatayer	78
Khuthra	59
Khutra makboos	72
Khyar ma' laban	19
Kibbet batata syamee	119
Kibby	51
Kibby labaneeyee	55
Kibby neeyee	52
Kibby bil saneeyee	55
Kibby samek	113
Kibby kishik	55
Kilwat ghanum mishwee	37
Kamaj	80
Knafee	102
Koosa ablama	67
Koosa makboos	76
Koosa mihshee	68
Koosa miqlee	126

Laban	7
Laban dahareej	3
Labanee	2
Labaneeyee lil koosa	67
Labaneeyee ma' roz	55
Laban imoo	36
Lahum mishwee	35
Lahum nee	1
Lahum wal mahrajan	31
Lahyoun	61
Laqmet il hilwee	107
Laqoum	129
Lefet lowz	102
Life makboos	73
Lubee	65
Maqloobee	66
Marquq	78
Ma' mool	104
Maza	1
Miglee	89
Miqtha makboos	73
Mlukheeyeh	14
Mowaseer	33
Mra-qud	80
Mulfoof mihshee	60
Munsoofee	127
Mushroob	87
Musakhan	44
Nbeeth	90
Qahweh	88
Qasabee imhamatha	34
Qilbee	136
Qarnabeet wa banadoora	61, 124
Qary dis ma' marqet	113
Qurban	134
Qawarma	38
Qroon ujwet yansoon	130
Qras mihshee	54
Qras miqlee	54
Qras ma' habesh	54
Qras mishwee ma' laban	54
Qras syamee	119
Qish'r bur-d-kan, limoon	94

Rishta	122
Roz eb haleeb	106
Roz eb sabanigh	125
Roz imfalfel	46
Roz ma' qiwanis	47
Roz ma' sha' reeyee	46
Ruhmee	136
Sabanigh imqala	126
Sabanigh ma' limoon	66
Sabanigh wa lahum	67
Salata	17
Salata baqdownis wa jowz	19
Salata hindbee	19
Salata batinjan	21
Salata khyar ma' laban	20
Salata jirjeeree	19
Salata il sane	19
Salata il shamunder	19
Salata khuthra	21
Salata syamee	17
Salatet fasoolya	17
Salatet sabanigh	19
Samek	110
Samek al qud ma' marqet	112
Samek barboor	112
Samek makhbooz	111
Samek mihshee	110
Samek Sultan Ibrahim	110
Samin imfaqis	45
Sane il buqqar	33
Sayedeeya	114
Sfeeha	83
Sheesh barak	33
Sheikh il mihshee	62
Shikreeyee	36
Shish kebab	35
Shouraba	11
Shourba il homos	11
Shourba kishik	12
Shourba il khuthra	12
Shourba djaj wa roz	11
Shraab	88
Shunkleesh	3
Shy ma' qirfee	89
Sharbet il toot	88

Shy ma' yansoon	89
Sikkar sumsum	107
Silliq mihshee	61
Sleeqa	137
Tabakh roohoo	124
Tabeekh	126
Tabooley - Suf	18
Tahini	4
Tajin	111
Talamee	80
Taratoor	4
Taratoor avocado	5
Teen ma'qood	93
Teen mihshee	93
Thilla'	36
Tutlee	109
Waraq inib makboos	76
Waraq inib mihshee	63
Waraq inib syamee	125
Waraq inib ma' habesh	63
Warbat il oshta	100
Wuz	42
Yubraq	60
Yubraq syamee	123
Yukhnee	35
Yukhnee lubee akhthar	123
Yukhnet batinjan	63
Yukhnet djaj	44
Zanaker	127
Zahra makboos	73
Zahra miqlee	61
Zahra qarnabeet	140
Zalabee	25
Zitoon	26
Zitoon akhthar	25
Zitoon aswad	25
Znood il banat	36

A platter of assorted Syrian dishes

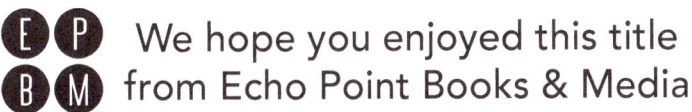 We hope you enjoyed this title from Echo Point Books & Media

Before Closing this Book, Two Good Things to Know

Buy Direct & Save

Go to www.echopointbooks.com (click "Our Titles" at top or click "For Echo Point Publishing" in the middle) to see our complete list of titles. We publish books on a wide variety of topics—from spirituality to auto repair.

Buy direct and save 10% at www.echopointbooks.com

DISCOUNT CODE: EPBUYER

Make Literary History and Earn $100 Plus Other Goodies Simply for Your Book Recommendation!

At Echo Point Books & Media we specialize in republishing out-of-print books that are united by one essential ingredient: high quality. Do you know of any great books that are no longer actively published? If so, please let us know. If we end up publishing your recommendation, you'll be adding a wee bit to literary culture and a bunch to our publishing efforts.

Here is how we will thank you:

- A free copy of the new version of your beloved book that includes acknowledgement of your skill as a sharp book scout.
- A free copy of another Echo Point title you like from echopointbooks.com.
- And, oh yes, we'll also send you a check for $100.

Since we publish an eclectic list of titles, we're interested in a wide range of books. So please don't be shy if you have obscure tastes or like books with a practical focus. To get a sense of what kind of books we publish, visit us at www.echopointbooks.com.

If you have a book that you think will work for us, send us an email at editorial@echopointbooks.com

www.ingramcontent.com/pod-product-compliance
Lightning Source LLC
Chambersburg PA
CBHW041243240426

43670CB00024B/2966